Transitions

Transitions are **S**uper **F**un
Activities that help any age
student shift or move into
the next part of the school
day in an organized way.

Editors
Cay McAninch, M.Ed.
Vikki Boatman, Ed.D.

Thank all of you for your dedicated support of this great university. As we begin to fill this new building with students, let us remember to 'Keep the Children Dancing, Learning, and Happy.'

James I. Perkins

Copyright ©2015
STEPHEN F. AUSTIN STATE UNIVERSITY PRESS
Manufactured in South Korea,
through Four Colour Print Group
All rights reserved
First edition
Second printing

This paper meets the requirements of
ANSI/NISO Z39.48 - 1992
(Permance of Paper)
Binding Materials have been
chosen for durability.

ISBN: 978-1-62288-109-3

A special thanks to Karen Frandsen of Karen's Kids Studio for the generous use of her images.
www.karenskidsstudio.com

TRANSITIONS is dedicated to Dr. Janice Pattillo who began this collection in the form of a handout for her students in the 1970's at Stephen F. Austin State University. Dr. Pattillo's dedication, insight, and leadership has been highly instrumental in the development of thousands of teachers. Her visions and desire for excellence in teaching have been crucial to the success and the philosophy embraced by the Elementary Education Department at Stephen F. Austin State University. Through her motivation and guidance, teachers are using *TRANSITIONS* to create positive learning atmospheres in classrooms across the United States as well as abroad.

Thank you, Dr. Pattillo, for loving children and encouraging thousands of teachers to strive to nurture, respect, and develop the whole child.

In honor of all teachers, past, present, and future.

Stephen F. Austin State University has a long history of lab schools. In 1969, the Elementary Education Department started a University Kindergarten. The school has grown into the Janice Pattillo Early Childhood Research Center that you see in the above picture. This facility houses infants through fifth-grade and the college classrooms/offices for elementary education. A booklet of Transitions

has been a part of the preparation of teachers since 1969, although it has been revised many times during the years. We hope you enjoy using these activities and embrace the subtle and powerful ways to help children learn as they gently change activities during their day.

Janice Pattillo, Ph.D.

Overview of this Book

ANY activity that helps students shift, move into the next part of the school day, or pay attention in an organized way can be considered a transition. The use of transitions helps **"GLUE"** the day together and aid in classroom management.

The **age of the child is an important consideration** when selecting which transitions to use in your classroom. Young children, as well as older ones, will gladly participate when the transition is *age and content appropriate*. Older children respond well to transitions that are not 'baby' sounding. Transitions specifically targeting older students will be found throughout the book. Of course, most transitions can be modified to use with any age and for multiple purposes.

Transitions in this book include: **capturing attention**, **waiting, moving, teaching, and dismissing.** As you try these and explore their use, it is important to remember you may use the same transition to accomplish different purposes. A transition used to gain attention may also work well for waiting or dismissal.

Throughout this book, you will find hints, tips, and suggestions from various teachers who have used transitions effectively in the classroom **with all ages of children**.

When first incorporating transitions into your day, try not to overwhelm yourself; start with one and go from there.

Cay McAninch, M. Ed.
Early Childhood Resource Room Coordinator
Early Childhood Lecturer
Stephen F. Austin State University

CONTENTS

CAPTURING ATTENTION

WAITING

MOVING

CLEAN UP

TEACHING

**PHONEMIC
AWARENESS**

DISMISSAL

TRANSITIONS-An Effective Classroom Management Tool

*Using **TRANSITIONS** throughout the day provides a way to support and promote positive behavior. Transitions provide a way for the teacher to effectively and positively maintain order.*

Setting a Positive Tone

*Using **TRANSITIONS** to get attention or give directions provides a positive way to state classroom expectations. For example, when children work independently in learning centers or in small groups, a song such as "Clean Up" provides a signal to all children in the classroom without the teacher having to raise his/her voice over the sounds of the various activities. This allows the teacher to use an appropriate teacher voice while providing guidance for behavior.*

Engaging Children/Preventing Disruptive Behavior

*Daily schedules for young children involve many changes of activities. Using **TRANSITIONS** provides a way to maintain order and limit disruptions during these changes. The teacher may use a song, a game, or a fingerplay to maintain children's attention as they move from one activity to another.*

While waiting for a few children to join the group, such as after washing hands or before a story, an active song maintains the attention of those children who are already at the rug, while providing an incentive for the other children to join the group.

Cueing

Using a song to cue children, for example, "5 Minutes to Clean Up," helps prepare the children for the shift in activity. When the Clean Up song is sung, children will be more likely to respond appropriately.

Reinforcing Positive Behavior

*Another way to use **TRANSITIONS** for management is to use the songs or activities to reinforce positive behavior. For example, when children come to the rug to join the group activity, use their name in a song to reinforce their behavior. Any song that involves using the children's names is useful for this.*

Also, to dismiss children to learning centers or outside play, use a song that dismisses children individually by name. This allows the teacher to first call children who have been participating appropriately in the activity.

Liz Vaughan, Ph.D.
Chair/Professor, ECRC
Stephen F. Austin State University

TRANSITIONS for the VERY YOUNG CHILD

Whether standing in line with Mom or Dad at the grocery store or waiting to get food for lunch at a childcare center or at home, children of all ages must learn to wait. Children must also move and go places they may not necessarily choose, and the use of transitions makes these times more manageable and fun.

Transitions for small babies are primarily a calming technique. Singing short songs or nursery rhymes help the babies settle down and anticipate what will happen next.

Ms. Melissa McCormack

As children grow, transitions are used to move them from place to place (inside to outside, room to room, activity to activity). Infants are much more apt to go somewhere willingly if it is fun or some sort of game. Transitions provide young children with some control over their world and introduce them to some sort of order.

In Toddler I we use transitions as an easy, fun way to get children to move from one activity to another. It's a way to get our Toddler's attention and get the whole class moving at the same time. We also use transitions while waiting for activities, such as washing hands for lunch. When the room gets louder than we would like, we use quieting transitions to reduce the noise level. Transitions can also be used to deliver instructions for classroom routines; when we want to clean up the room and move into another activity, we sing the same group of songs everyday, so that the Toddlers know what is expected of them.

Ms. Louann Williams, Ms. Heather Verell, and Ginny Love

Transitions are a much more appropriate option than 'yelling' or trying to "talk over" a child, because children are more receptive to transitions. Transitions are a quick way to capture or regain a child's attention when the child is distracted. Asking children to help sing a song, locate a body part, or use a finger play that ends with the children's hands in their lap, is a quick way to make sure the children are focused and on task.

In a Pre-K classroom, transitions are used all day, every day. Transitions are used to capture the children's attention, to move children from one place to another, to keep the children occupied while waiting, to teach new concepts or practice old ones, and to give reminders. Transitions help to keep the classroom room running efficiently and smoothly in a fun and organized way. Making transitions fun helps to keep the children excited and occupied while learning at the same time.

Ms. Emily Tacquard, Pre K II Teacher

Using transitions with any age child, even the very young child, will make a positive difference in the flow of each moment of the day. Transitions also help to prepare children for the next stage of their learning and development.

Loving and learning together makes all the difference in the world!

Lori M. Harkness, M.Ed.
Early Childhood Laboratory, Director
Stephen F. Austin State University

Teachers have many tools in their **instructional tool box.** Transitions are a perfect example. Instructional time in the classroom is a teacher's most valuable commodity, and efficient use of this time must be *intentional* and *purposeful*.

©*KGF*

Often, valuable time is lost when students are returning to the classroom from lunch, the restroom, extracurricular classes, or when changing from one activity to another. Instead of waiting for all students to return before beginning a new lesson, use a teaching transition. Review or strengthen recent concepts by engaging students in short **instructional moments.** Increase students' productive thinking skills by using these 'wait' times to analyze current topics of study. Using instructional transitions can also strengthen listening skills, extend vocabulary and verbal fluency, and support flexible thinking.

Students use visual, auditory, and kinesthetic modalities to process information. Encouraging students to talk and move, transitions offer a perfect opportunity for auditory and kinesthetic learners. Many students need to **hear themselves** repeat information while **movement may be the key** for other students. However, it is the teacher's responsibility to match transition types with student needs.

Spending just two minutes a day engaged in an instructional transition will replace 6 hours of 'down time' in a child's school year! What teacher can't use an extra 6 hours of instructional time? Think of all the non-instructional times during a day and multiply that by 180 days. You really can "get it all in" if you make a point of turning non-instructional time into instructional time through the use of transitions.

Classroom conflict is often the result of too much non-instructional time. Providing appropriate instructional activity during transition times will **strengthen academic success** while **reducing conflict**. Using intentional transitions puts the teacher in control of 'down time' and provides acceptable avenues for talking and movement in the classroom.

Look for specific examples of ways to use instructional transitions in this book.

Carolyn Davis, Ph.D.
Early Childhood Undergraduate Coordinator
Stephen F. Austin State University

TRANSITIONS for the YOUNG CHILD

Transitions are positive and cheerful ways of moving any age children from one activity to another. They help teachers use every minute of every day for learning while avoiding "wait time" which results in "lost time." Transitions occupy hands, minds, and bodies. By such involvement, you will find a direct correlation between time well spent and positive classroom management. The use, or lack thereof, of transitions will make OR break your entire day.

A lot of extra time or materials are not needed to use transitions. The teacher will find that transitions actually save time. Transitions are nothing more than SOMETHING CONSTRUCTIVE (and educational) to keep children involved. Quite simply, they are rhymes, fingerplays, chants, and songs used to engage learners.

How much better it is to capture children's attention with a fingerplay, song, or chant rather than to scold, saying, "Shhhh, be quiet!" "Pay attention" or "Everybody sit down!" When teachers use transitions children become involved, interested, and engaged in what the teacher is doing allowing the teacher to be "in control" in a child-centered manner.

After using transitions for one week, if the teacher finds himself or herself acting as a referee or policeman/woman, constantly nagging and scolding children, perhaps he/she is not effectively using transitions. If this happens, closely examine how you are implementing them.

When using transitions, there are some important pointers to remember.

1. In the beginning, <u>have a game plan</u>. Know what transitions you are going to use and at what times. Have the transitions available on a card (in sequenced order) to serve as a guideline for each day of the week until you become familiar with them.

2. <u>Change the words to fit the needs of the group</u>. If you are waiting on four friends, sing about four friends. If you are waiting on one friend, use her name.

3. <u>Utilize children's names when possible</u>. This helps keep children focused and interested. Just make sure you use all names equally and that you do not single out one child.

4. ALWAYS <u>end with children in a quiet and controlled situation</u>: hands in lap, sitting down, or standing quietly.

5. There are no such things as "written in blood" transitions. <u>Make up transitions that fit your children's needs</u>. A song sung for group music can also be a transition.

6. <u>Singing transitions seems to work best for young children</u>, particularly when capturing or regaining their attention. A singing voice is louder than a talking voice and it is heard more easily. <u>Chants work well with older children</u>.

7. When possible, <u>use hand and body movements</u>. This helps children keep their hands to themselves and away from other children. Research also shows that physical activity actually helps us learn better.

8. Most important of all, **<u>USE TRANSITIONS</u>**!! They will absolutely MAKE or BREAK your day. Transitions are great ways of keeping the class in order while reinforcing learned skills.

   This book contains a limited set of transitions. It provides examples of transitions and when to use them. Remember that no single transition is used solely in one part of the day. A variety of transitions should be used at a variety of times.

   When I first began to understand the concept of "transitions," I thought only certain songs, chants and activities could be used at designated times. In reality, any song, chant, rap, or activity can be used as a transition throughout the day and changed to meet children's needs.

Be creative! Create your own transitions using familiar tunes. See the examples set to the tune of *Row, Row, Row, Your Boat.*

Capturing/Regaining Attention

We're coming to the rug, we're coming to the rug. We're coming to the rug, so give yourself a hug.

Clean-Up

Clean, clean, clean right up. Clean your center now. Clean, clean, clean right up. Come and join us now.

Dismissal

Line up if you will, line up if you will. We are going to eat lunch. Come along and munch.

Moving

Take one giant step, now take two more please. This time baby steps, baby steps like these.

Waiting

Clap, clap, clap your hands, clap above your head. Clap, clap, clap your hands, clap below your knees.

As you can see, several of the "commands" are simple and similar. It is just a matter of being creative and using words that will stretch your children's minds, vocabularies, and thinking skills. There are not "right" or "wrong" transitions when you use them appropriately to occupy, stretch, and encourage children… regardless of their age.

The misnomer that upper elementary children do not like to sing is false. I've been in fourth grade classrooms where children love to sing. The teacher's attitude about singing definitely impacts the children.

Give transitions a try for one week. If they do not significantly impact your classroom management, I want to know!!

Vikki Boatman, Ed.D.
Early Childhood Graduate Coordinator
Stephen F. Austin State University

Happy Transitioning:)

Transitions Can Teach/Assess/Review

A **dismissal transition** is a great way to check for understanding at the end of a lesson or to review previously studied material while your students are **waiting** to begin something new. Transitions are a wonderful way to **learn social knowledge** (telling time, identifying shapes, naming states or continents, etc.)

The trick to transitions is to keep a fast **pace,** so that no one gets bored waiting for a turn. Be sure to challenge every student to his or her potential. In other words, be prepared with your transition!

Remember, students may respond **individually**, as a **pair**, or as a **small/whole group**. Transitions can be used to **teach, review,** and **assess** material.

TEACHING

A teacher might have a clock with movable hands to help students **learn** to tell time. A familiar chant to *Oh Do You Know the Muffin Man* could be sung as the time on the clock was shown to a student/s.

> "Tell what time it is. (Show one child the clock). Change the time, "What time is it now?" (show a different child). Change the time, "What time is it?" (continue to change the time for each new clock time question while moving from child to child quickly for an answer). Change the time, "Oh do you know what time it is?" change the time, "On my clock?"

This would quickly continue until all students have had a turn individually or in pairs. What a fun way to **teach/review** telling time!

ASSESSING

A recent kindergarten lesson on **ending sounds** used the following transition to dismiss the students.

> Name the ending sound that you hear.... bat, great, foot.
> *The teacher points to two students to answer and then they leave the group for the next activity.*
> Name the ending sound that you hear.... hop, shape, trip.
> *The teacher again points to two students to answer and be dismissed. The transition continues until all have been dismissed, allowing her to assess each student.*

REVIEWING

A first or second grade class might use **Name the Number** as a transition to **review** concepts. As the students answer and think, they are also reviewing.

> *"Name the number just before ___."*
> *"Name the number just after ___."*
> *"Name a number between ___ and ___."*
> *"Name an odd number between ___ and ___."*
> *"Odd or Even? 23"*
> *"Name a number greater than ___."*
> *"Name a number less than ____?"*
> *"Name a number greater than ___ but less than ____."*
> *"Name a multiple of 4."*

WHO GETS WHAT QUESTION FIRST?

If your students are practicing a particularly new or difficult skill, begin the transition by calling on some of the more adept students, allowing the struggling students to hear the skill being used before taking a turn.

If it is a skill which can be adjusted up or down in difficulty level, randomly allow turns, thinking through your adjustment of the transition based on individual needs.

As you plan these teaching, assessing, reviewing transitions with your lessons, I think you will discover their usefulness in the classroom and how they can be a wonderful classroom management aid.

Lysa Hagan, M. Ed.
SFA Charter School CEO
Stephen F. Austin State University

©KGF

Sponge Activities

**Just as a sponge "soaks" up liquids,
sponge activities "soak" up drops
of time with students.**

For instance, I know many of my students need more practice with prefixes and suffixes. So ... I finish with my read aloud a few minutes early and it is not quite time to go to lunch. Instead of letting my students sit idle or have them play the quiet game, I will play the opposite game, " I say, you say."

> **I say, "Successful, you say _____ (unsuccessful)."**
> **I say, "Happy, you say _____ (unhappy)."**
>
> **I say, "Walk, you say _____ (walking)(walked)(walks)."**
> **I say, "Run, you say _____ (ran)."**

My students are not just practicing and applying these skills at this time. I can use this sponge activity for assessment, seeing who can and who can't. I may even have my tablet close by to write an anecdotal record of the skills observed or my checklist in hand to record the application of those skills.

The above activity could be used for waiting, capturing attention, or a dismissal activity. As you find transitions in the various sections in this book, remember not to limit their use to that area only.

With thought and practice, you too, will find yourself choosing sponge activities that highlight concepts needed to be taught or practiced.

**We hope you use the transitions in this book to
"soak" up more instructional
time for your students.**

Cay McAninch, M.Ed.
Early Childhood Resource Room Coordinator
Stephen F. Austin State University

Capturing Attention

SFA

©KGF

"Attention-getting" transitions can be used to gain the attention of any age child at anytime of the day. Use these 'attention getters' as needed before or during any activity to regain attention or to refocus students.

Teacher Talk

The students love **2,4,6,8** because they get to finish the chant after you start it. It gets their attention and they have fun.

Natalie Cardenas
5th SFA Charter School
SFASU 2009

2,4,6,8

Teacher: 2,4
Students:6,8,
Ms. _____'s class is super great!

If You Are Listening

If you are listening, touch your _____.

   body parts: Spanish- cabeza, umbros, boca, dientes, nariz, orejas, pello, etc. OR higher level words- spine, temple, calf, instep, etc. AVOID the obvious- head, eyes, toes, etc.

If you are listening, clap ____ times.

   clapping: Spanish- uno, dos, tres, quatro, etc.

If you are listening, spell _____.

   spelling words: practice spelling words for the week.

Be creative and make up your own or let the children help you.

©Karen's Kids

Teacher Talk

*This transition, **Got Soul**, works well with older students to regain their attention during any time of the day.*

Holli Zawlocki- 5th grade
SFA Charter School
SFASU 1994

Got Soul

Teacher says, "Hey"
Class replies, "Ho --- Ms. Holli's class got soul. Say what?"

Variations:

Teacher says, "Hands go up!"
Class replies, "Mouths go shut!"

Teacher says, "Give me 5!"
Children put their hands in the air.

Teacher says, "Paws"
Children put their hands in the air.

Clap Your Hands

Clap your hands, clap your hands, clap them just like me.
Touch your fingers, touch your fingers, touch them just like me.
Shake your head, shake your head, shake it just like me.
Clap your hands, clap your hands, now let them quiet be.

Teacher Talk

*We use this sign, **"L"** when on the rug, in line, any time any member of the class feels that we need a reminder to "check ourselves."*

Lauree Hayes - 1st grade
Charter School
SFASU 1982 and 1988

L   "L"

This upper case L is made by using your thumb and index finger when facing your students.

It stands for, "LOOK, LISTEN, LEARN."

Open, Shut Them

Open, shut them. Open, shut them. Give a little clap,
And put them on your lap.

Creep them, creep them, slowly to your rosy cheeks.
Open wide your shiny eyes and through your fingers peep.

Open, shut them. Open, shut them. To your shoulders fly.
Let them flutter like the birdies, flutter to the sky.

Falling, falling. Slowly downward, nearly to the ground.
Quickly raise them, up so high. Twirling round and round.

Open, shut them. Open, shut them. Give a little clap.
Open, shut them. Open, shut them. Put them in your lap.

Teacher Talk

*I frequently change the words to familiar transitions or think of fun new ones. For example, in place of turning off the lights to get students attention or screaming at them, I use this transition, **Change It**. It can be used any time, any where, and changed with the seasons, or content being taught to get children to **STOP, LOOK,** and **LISTEN**.*

Cathy May – Kindergarten
Shawnee Trail Elementary, Frisco
SFASU 2001

Change It

Teacher says: "Bingo."
Children say: "B-I-N-G-O, B-I-N-G-O, B-I-N-G-O,
And Bingo was his name-O."

Students know after they are finished they should be stopped, still, and listening to what I have to say.

Variations: As the year progresses, we add more variations.

Teacher says: "Here puppy."
Children: The children stop their words and movements then bark
three times at me.

Teacher says: "Santa."
Children: They hold their tummies and say "HO! HO! HO!"

Teacher says: "Funny bunny"
Children: The children hop 3 times and freeze.

Teacher says: "Summer's coming"
Children: "Hip Hip Hooray!"

Teacher says: "Rectangle"
Children: Draw in the air and say, "Has 4 sides."

A Circle We Will Make
(To the tune of *Farmer in the Dell*)

A circle we will make!
A circle we will make!
Hi-ho the dairy-o,
A circle we will make.

The circle will go fast,
The circle will go fast,
Hi-ho the dairy-o,
The circle will go fast.

Variations: go slow, jump, slide, etc.

Busy Fingers
(To the tune of *Mulberry Bush*)

This is the way my fingers stand, my fingers stand, my fingers stand.
This is the way my fingers stand, so early in the morning.
(or … in the afternoon) [Open one hand palm up. With the other hand, hold up two fingers. Turn them down to stand on your palm.]

This is the way my fingers dance, my fingers dance, my fingers dance.
This is the way my fingers dance, so early in the morning.
[Move two fingers back-and-forth across open palm.]

This is the way I fold my hands, fold my hands, fold my hands.
This is the way I fold my hands so they can go to rest.
[Fold hands and place in lap.]

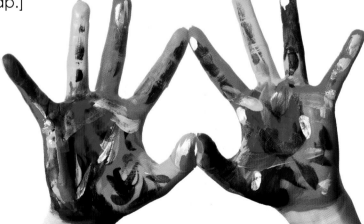

Do You Know What Time it Is?
(To the tune of *Muffin Man*)

Oh, do you know what time it is, what time it is, what time it is?
Oh, do you know what time it is? It's <u>story</u> time you see.

Variation: Fill in the blank with the activity in which children are to engage:
...come to the rug.
...read a book.

Grandpa's Glasses

Here are Grandpa's glasses.
Here is Grandpa's hat.
Here's the way he folds his arms
And here's the way he sat.

Here are Grandma's glasses.
Here is Grandma's cap.
Here is the way she folds her hands
And lays them in her lap.

Won't You Come and Sit Right Here?
(To the tune of *Mary Had a Little Lamb*)

Won't you come and sit right here?
Sit right here? Sit right here?
Won't you come and sit right here?
To hear our story now.

Variations: stand, jump, to come and eat your lunch, to listen to our friend, etc.

©KGF

Teacher Talk

One of my class's favorite transitions is **I Wiggle My Fingers** because they get the chance to wiggle and be silly for a moment on the carpet. Using transitions in my classroom has helped to make my days run smoother and to not lose a moment of teaching time.

Brittany Tanner-Pre-K
Barrow Elementary
SFASU 2008

I Wiggle My Fingers

I wiggle my fingers, I wiggle my toes.
I wiggle my shoulders, I wiggle my nose.
Now no more wiggles are left in me.
So I will sit still, as still as can be.

I'll Know You are Listening

I'll know you are listening because I will see friends...

...with their hands on their _____ (head, shoulders, table top, etc.)

...standing quietly.

...looking at me.

...clap 3 times, jump once.

It is Time to Make a Circle
(To the tune of *Twinkle, Twinkle, Little Star*)

Let us make a circle now.
Find your place and take a bow.
Wave your hands: one, two, three.
Clap your hands and touch your knee.
It is time to make a circle,
Find your place and take a bow.

Teacher Talk

After parties, activities, or active times, **Tommy Thumb** *is an excellent way to calm children down, to get them focused, and ready to listen. It can be chanted or sung. It has a sweet tune.*

Cherly Athey
SFASU 1979 and 1985

Tommy Thumb

Tommy Thumb is up and Tommy Thumb is down.
(Hold both thumbs in the air.)

Tommy Thumb is dancing all around the town.
(Make thumbs dance around in the air.)

Dance him on your shoulders; dance him on your head.
(Dance thumbs on shoulders and head.)

Dance him on your knees and tuck him into bed.
(Dance thumbs on your knees and tuck thumbs under each arm.)

Continue same words as above, substituting the various fingers using the
following names:
Peter Pointer
Toby Tall Man
Ruby Ring
Baby Finger
Finger Family

Last verse will be the whole family of fingers. Throughout the last verse, slow the rhythm down and continue to lower your voice until you are slowly whispering…and tuck them into bed (wrap hand around fingers).

Variations: Try substituting daddy, grandma, grandpa, or child's name for mommy. Any time you use a child's name in a transition, it is a real attention grabber!

Teacher Talk

*One of my favorite ways to teach listening skills involves the use of movement and verbal directions. Children often copy the movement of others or the teacher without listening carefully. This transition, **If You Can Hear**, allows for movement but encourages active listening.*

Carolyn Davis
Elementary Education Department
SFASU 1977 and 1982

If You Can Hear

If you can hear my words, put your hands on your head.
(teacher puts hands on stomach)
If you can hear my words, put your hands on your knees.
(teacher puts hands on ears)

Variations:

If you can hear my words, put your hands on your clavicle, femur, forehead, patella, scalp . . . (Say these quickly - when teaching the body parts the teacher touches the correct body part - later just name the parts.)

If you can hear my words, put your **eyes** on the door, on the ceiling, on the globe, on the math center, on the . . . . (Say these quickly; the point is to get everyone focused quickly. The last command should be 'on me.')

It is also fun to spell the object or body part being named.

One, Two, Three, Eyes on Me

One, two, three!
Eyes on me!
Won't you listen to me please?

One, two, three.
Eyes on me.

For older students: "1-2-3 eyes on me"

I Say... You Say ...

Teacher: "I say Charter, you say School" – " Charter"
Students: "School"
  Teacher: "Charter"
  Students: "School"

Variations:
Teacher: "I say Pre-K , you say – 2" "Pre-K"
Students: "2"
  Teacher: "Pre-K"
  Students: "2"

Teacher: "I say sounds , you say off" – "sounds"
Students: "off"
  Teacher: "sounds"
  Students: "off"

Only One Can Talk at a Time

Only one can talk at a time
So this is what I'll do.
I'll sit and listen quietly
Until <u>everyone</u> is through.

Variation: Substitute "everyone" with the name of the child who is talking.

Teacher Talk

Two Fat Sausages is a great way to get children to focus. The different voices attract the children's attention and help them focus on your words. The different voice levels, from high to low and loud to soft, really help children prepare to listen.

Karen Farris – Pre-K II
SFA Lab School
SFASU 1987 and 1999

Two Fat Sausages

(in **medium size voice** in rhythmic pattern chant)
> **2 fat sausages sizzling in a pan.**
> **1 went "pop".** (pop sound with finger on side mouth)
> **And the other went "bam".** (clap)

(in **LOUD size voice** in rhythmic pattern chant)
> **2 fat sausages sizzling in a pan.**
> **1 went "pop".** (pop sound with finger on side mouth)
> **And the other went "bam".** (clap really loud)

(in **baby size voice** in rhythmic pattern chant)
> **2 baby sausages sizzling in a pan.**
> **1 went "pop".** (pop sound with finger on side mouth)
> **And the other went "bam".** (clap with pinky fingers)

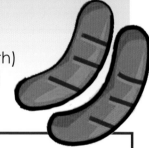

This is the Way We Make a Circle
(To the tune of *Mulberry Bush*)

This is the way we make a circle, make a circle, make a circle.
This is the way we make a circle so early in the morning.

This is the way we march and march; march and march; march and march.
This is the way we march and march; so early in the morning.

Change actions and time of day to fit your needs.

Teacher Talk

Are You Listening? is a classic that I modified in my kindergarten classroom. Each verse can be changed so the children are allowed to respond in loud or quiet voices, and each of the actions can be changed to facilitate various behaviors. (Jump up and down, turn around, put your hands on your head, put your pencil on the table, line up at the door, etc.) It is a great way to redirect off-task behaviors or to gain the attention of the group in a positive manner.

Tracey Hasbun
Elementary Education Department
SFASU 1993 and 2003

Are You Listening?
(To the tune of *Frere Jacques*)

Teacher: Are you listening? If you're listening, say, "Yes, we are."
Students: "Yes, we are."
Teacher: Do a little wiggling and a little jiggling, put your hands on your head.
Teacher: Are you listening? If you're listening, whisper, "Yes, we are."
Students: "Yes, we are."
Teacher: "Put your bottom on the rug, give yourself a great big hug, put your hands in your lap.

My Hands

My hands upon my head I place, on my shoulders, on my face.
On my waist and by my side, and then behind my back they hide.
I let my fingers fly, fly, fly. I try to touch the sky, sky, sky.
I clap my hands with one, two, three, And now I fold them quietly.

Teacher Talk

Sometimes songs and transitions grow out of those unplanned but teachable moments. During an author study of Marc Brown, author of the Arthur series, a discussion about aardvarks developed. I challenged my kindergarteners to research the subject and see what they could find out about the subject of Brown's books. The next day Colton returned to school with a ball of yarn cut to the length of a mature aardvark from the tip of its nose to the tip of its tail. We stretched the yarn across the classroom and then the students shared their discoveries.

*We used the information gathered to write a song, **Aardvark,** to help us remember what we had discussed. The students drew pictures of the story book character, and we used the artwork to decorate a song card. This became one of our favorite transitions as we prepared to read new Marc Brown books.*

Carolyn Davis
Elementary Education Department
SFASU 1977 and 1982

Aardvark
(To the Tune of *Are You Sleeping?*)

A-A-R-D, V-A-R-K
That spells aardvark,
That spells aardvark.

An aardvark is a mammal,
An aardvark is a mammal,
They have fur,
They have fur.

Aardvarks are nocturnal,
Aardvarks are nocturnal,
They sleep at night,
They sleep at night.

Aardvarks live in Africa,
Aardvarks live in Africa,
That's a continent,
That's a continent.

Teacher Talk

*This activity, **Bomp Bomp**, is quick and can be done in a split second with ages 2-82. I first heard it from the computer lab teacher in our school. It quickly became one of my favorites. When you try it, I think you will see why!*

Cay McAninch
Elementary Education Department
SFASU 1978 and 1982

Bomp Bomp

Teacher says: "Bomp badda bomp bomp."
Students answer: "Bomp bomp!"

Time for Story Time
(To the tune of *Mulberry Bush*)

Now it's time for story time, story time, story time.
Now it's time for story time, It's story time right now.

Story Time Rhyme

Sometimes my hands are by my side, *(place hands at side)*
Sometimes behind my back they hide. *(place hands behind back)*

Sometimes I wiggle my fingers so!
I shake them fast (*shake hands quickly*).
I shake them slow (*shake hands slowly*).

Sometimes my hands go clap, clap, clap, *(hands clap)*
And then I lay them in my lap. *(fold hands and place in lap)*

Now they are as quiet, as quiet can be,
Because it's story time, you see.

Teacher Talk

This activity, **ATTENTION**, is great for calming a roomful of active older students quickly. They find it fun to say and immediately look MY way.

Jan Wisener - 4th grade
SFA Charter School
SFASU 1984 and 1986

ATT - ENT - I - O - N

Teacher says: the word..."ATTENTION"(pause)
Students Spell: "ATT - ENT - I - O - N
I'VE GOT YOURS
YOU'VE GOT MINE
SO LET'S – BEGIN."

Two Little Hands

Two little hands go clap, clap, clap.
Two little feet go tap, tap, tap.
One little body turns around.
One little body sits quietly down.

Two little feet go jump, jump, jump.
Two little fists go thump, thump, thump.
Each little child turns around, round, round.
Then each little child sits quietly down.

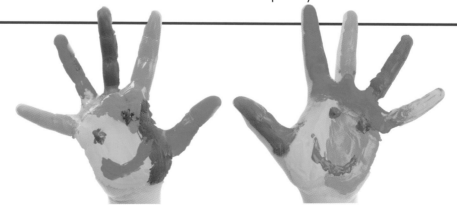

Teacher Talk

Transitions are wonderful for teachers, especially those teachers who are new. My first year I quickly discovered that students and teachers love to sing and dance. **Up, Down** *is a fun song that I made up to have my students come to the rug in the mornings. It helps release all that morning energy as we up, down, and finally sit on the ground for a story. The teacher will start singing, and while singing, he and his students will reach up for the sky and down for the ground. He then has them move and groove to where he needs them. Teachers can sing it as long as they need, and when the students finally get to where the teacher wants them, he will sing the last line. Once the students have learned the song, watch them sing along.*

William Weeks - 1st Grade
Huntington Elem.
SFASU 2008

Up, Down

When I'm up, down, touch the ground it puts me in the mood
Up, down, touch the ground in the mood {clap,clap} to move
When I'm up, down, I have found
I improve my mood (clap,clap) when I groove.

When I'm up, down, touch the ground it puts me in the mood
Up, down, touch the ground in the mood (clap,clap) to move
When I'm up, down, turn around then I (clap, clap) sit down.

Teacher Talk

Firecracker is great to use when I need to get the students' attention. The 3rd graders respond well to this and are ready to listen when the firecracker is finished.

Jeri Meredith
SFASU 1994 and 2000

Firecracker

Teacher says: "Firecracker, firecracker."

Students say: "1-2-3" They make a firecracker with their hands and sounds. When the firecracker is finished...after a few seconds...the students should be still and looking and listening to the teacher."

Teacher Talk

This transition is great when my friends forget to put their sounds away. It is very quick and easy to sing. It is especially helpful when a Pre-K II friend is sharing because you can insert the friend's name. Sometimes the children join in and sing with me!

Emily Wilson Pre-K II
SFA Lab School
SFASU 2008 and 2011

It's My Turn

"It's my turn to talk and your turn to listen."
"It's _____ (child's name) turn to talk and your turn to listen."

Teacher Talk

I use ¿Como se llama? when calling students to the rug. It is a Spanish transtion used as an echo chant. I begin with a Spanish version, and then the students repeat the same question. I then sing the English translation, and the students repeat. The child I point to repeats his/her answer.

**Chris Rodriguez – Kindergarten
SFASU**

¿Como se llama?

Teacher says: "¿Como se llama?"
Class echoes: "¿Como se llama?"
Teacher says: "What's your name?"
Class echoes: "What's your name?"
That student says: "Me llamo _____(name)?"
Class echoes: "Me llamo _____(name)?"
That student says: "That's my name!"
Class says: "That's his name."

Variation: *Choose a special pointer to tap friend or a sombrero to pass around.*

Use different question: *"¿Como estas?" How are you?*
Answer: *"Estoy bien." I am fine.*

We're Glad to be Together
(To the tune of *Mulberry Bush*)

We're glad to be together, together, together.
We're glad to be together, together again.
There's Brandon and Brady and Holly and Aimee.
We're glad to be together again in our school.

Teacher Talk

*Many teachers use the **I Say...You Say...** method for capturing attention. This method can be utilized with upper elementary students to reinforce content vocabulary while capturing attention.*

Erica S. Dillard
Nacogdoches Independent School District
SFASU 1996 and 2001

I Say...You Say...Content Focus

Example 1-Science:
I Say Producer; You Say Consumer. Producer, Consumer, Producer, Consumer.

Example 2-Social Studies:
I Say Texas, You Say Austin. Texas, Austin, Texas, Austin.

Example 3-Economics:
I Say Supply, You Say Demand. Supply, Demand, Supply, Demand.

Example 4-Mathematics:
I Say Product, You Say Multiply. Product, Multiply, Product, Multiply.

Where is Charity?
(To the tune of *Where is Thumbkin?*)

Teacher:	Where is Charity? Where is Charity?
Charity:	Here I am. Here I am.
Teacher:	Won't you come and join us?
	Won't you come and join us?
Charity:	Yes, I will. Yes, I will.
Teacher:	Where is Charity? Where is Charity?
Charity:	Here I am. Here I am.
Teacher:	Please stand up. Please stand up.
	Do a little jumping. Do a little jumping.
	Come over here. Come over here.

Waiting

Idle students in a classroom can pose problems for teachers. The use of games, songs, chants, thinking activities, etc., during waiting times can help any age child remain actively engaged as they are

listening,
learning, and
DOING.

Cloud Ride

Everyone lies on his or her back.

Be careful not to rock or you'll tip the cloud.
Wave 'hello' to the little birdies.
Put on your sunglasses.
Oh, it is beginning to rain. Up with your umbrellas.
Hold on! An airplane is swooshing by.
It's getting chilly up here. Wrap up in a blanket.

The teacher can add other movements as she chooses.

Teacher Talk

When I do this in pre-k, I do it as they are coming to the rug. It can even be done on the playground. The children will come up to me and point to their clothes saying "BLUE," "PINK." They are so excited when it is their turn. It can also be done when the younger students are getting out of control.

**Maggie Brown - Infant – Pre-K II
SFA Lab School**

Little Red Box

If I had a little _____ box
(use the color of the clothes that child is wearing)
to put _____ in it.
(use the name of a child you are singing about)
I'd take her/him out and kiss, kiss, kiss, and put him/her back again.

**Repeat using different colors and names.
Use shapes, too.**

Teacher Talk

*Before going on a **Bear Hunt**, remember to pack your lunch (what did you pack for lunch?), your flashlight, and your towel – in your back pack. You may even stop along the way to look in the river or under the bridge…what do you see? You might find a horse to ride – it might gallop, walk, or run. You might find a bumpy old tractor to ride on. Use your imagination each time you go. You will be amazed at what kind of "bear hunting" trips the children invent.*

Cay McAninch – SFASU
Elementary Education Department
SFASU 1978 and 1982

Bear Hunt

We're going on a bear hunt. (*Children echo each line.*)
We're coming to a bridge.
We can't go around it.
We can't go under it.
We'll have to go over it.

We're coming to …..
wheat field
bridge
mountains
river
sticker patch

We're coming to a cave. (*slow the rhythm*)
We can't go around it.
We can't go under it.
We'll have to go in it.

It's dark in here. I see two big eyes. I feel a cold, cold nose.
I feel big sharp teeth. IT'S A BEAR! RUN!

Travel back through your adventure in reverse order until you get back home.

Button Factory

Hi! My name is Jim. I have a wife, three kids, and I work in a button factory.
The other day, my boss said, "Jim, are you busy?"
I said, "No."
He said, "Turn the button with your _____."

1. right hand
2. left hand
3. right foot
4. left foot
5. head
6. tongue

Final verse:
Hi! My name is Jim. I have a wife, three kids, and I work in a button factory.
The other day, my boss said, "Jim, are you busy?"
I said, "YES!!"
And I sat right down.

Animal Imitation

One child draws a card from the box/can. Each card has a familiar animal picture. The child imitates the animal's movements and sounds. Children on the rug try to guess the animal. The child who guesses the animal may act out the next animal OR the child/teacher can call on a friend to be next.

*This transition is a fun way to add literacy and math to those times when children have to wait. **Kiss Your Brain** could be used when children are gathering for a small or large group experience or when you have an unexpected wait time. It is quick, fun, and works well for older children, too.*

Brenda Bowline – Pre-K II
SFA Lab School
SFASU 2005

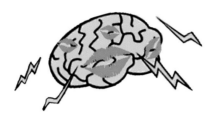

Kiss Your Brain

Sets of cards with questions on them are prepared and kept in a "Kiss Your Brain Jar." With younger children, I ask questions about animals, rhyming words, simple math questions, and phonemic awareness questions. The cards are very easily made by putting the questions on labels and then putting the labels on index cards. I color code the type of question by putting them on colored index cards, e.g., questions about animals on blue cards, phonemic awareness questions on pink cards, and math questions on yellow cards.

The teacher pulls a card out of the jar
and asks, "Can you name an animal that swims?"
The child answers, "A turtle can swim."
Teacher says, "Kiss your brain!"

Variations: "Kiss Your Brain" could be easily adapted to older children by asking content related questions. With younger children, you can also ask questions about nursery rhymes, e.g., "Who sat on a tuffet and ate curds and whey?"

Teacher Talk

We use the CD player on the first day of class to demonstrate and equate the various volumes and practice them. We come to a consensus that this is reasonable and will help us all do our best work, be happy, and successful. It has worked like a charm!

Lauree Hayes – 1st Grade
SFASU 1982 and 1988
SFA Charter School

Volumes

0 = silent
1 = whisper
2= appropriate for partners
3 = appropriate for small groups
4/5 = presenting/ whole group
6 – 10 = outside only

Chaquita Banana

Chaquita Banana!!
Go bananas!! Go, go, bananas
Go bananas!! Go, go, bananas
Go bananas!! Go, go, bananas
Go bananas!! Go, go, bananas
Lean to the left
Lean to the right
Peel your banana and
Take a bite!

Teacher Talk

Mystery Envelope *is good to use when children are gathering and waiting for small or large group experiences to begin. Children love to listen to clues and try to figure out what is in the envelope. It really holds their attention!*

Brenda Bowline – Pre-K II
SFA Lab School

Mystery Envelope

Find interesting pictures such as animals or vehicles to put inside large, 9 X 12 envelopes. On the outside of the envelope, write 5 or 6 clues to read to the children as they try to guess what is inside the envelope. Start with very general clues and get more specific with each additional clue. I ask the children to show me they have a guess by signaling with a quiet "yes" sign. The child raises his hand, gives the sign for yes, and puts a finger on his lips to remind him to wait his turn to talk.

For a mystery envelope with a picture of a squirrel inside:
Teacher says -   1. It is an animal.
                                2. It has fur.
                                3. It has four legs.
                                4. It lives in trees.
                                5. It has a bushy tail.
                                6. It likes to eat nuts.

Children - guess after each clue.

Variations: This transition could easily be adapted for older children by having pictures of presidents or science related pictures.

Clap Your Hands
(To the tune of Row, Row, Row Your Boat)

Clap, clap, clap your hands.
Clap you hands together.
Clap, clap, clap your hands.
Clap your hands together.

Change **clap** to **pat**, **roll**, etc.
Change **hands** to **feet** and **stomp**, **tap**, etc.
Change **feet** to **head** and **nod**, **shake**, etc.

©KGF

Mac-a-Lina Pack-a-Lina

Oh, she had two hairs on her head. One was alive and the other was dead.

CHORUS: Oh, Mack-a-lina, Pack-a-lina, Reubensteiner, Einer, Diner, Hokum, Pokum Locum was her naaaaaaaame!

She had two eyes, in her head. One was purple and the other was red. (CHORUS)
She had two holes in her nose. One was open and the other was closed. (CHORUS)
She had two teeth in her mouth. One pointed north and the other pointed south. (CHORUS)
She had two feet. She swam like a rock. When she hit the bottom you could hear her on the top. (CHORUS)

Sing last verse very slowly.

A ten-ton truck hit Mac-a-lina!
The man had to buy him a new ma-china!
CHORUS: Regular speed.

Teacher Talk

Keep'em Guessing! *That's what keeps my first graders involved and interested when it comes to group time on the rug. I have a small treasure chest on the shelf close by filled with props or "treasures" to use for transitions or "sponge activities." This is very effective because of the proximity and the spontaneity of the activities. You will find you can use them for any type of transition you need. Waiting, dismissal, content, etc. The possibilities are never ending!*

Just remember to put each treasure back where it belongs and keep those young inquiring minds wondering what comes next!

Jana Baker McCall – Jacksonville I.S.D.
Stephen F. Austin 1982
University of Houston 1986

"Keep'em Guessing!"

Some of the students' favorite treasures include:

a beanie baby bee - used for the "Bee Bee Bumble Bee" dismissal transition

a large button - used for "Button Button Who Has The Button" dismissal transition

rhinestone sunglasses - used for "I Spy" waiting transition

squish ball - used for "Sparkle" or tossing for responses during review of the day

a fun foam sandwich used for "Peanut Peanut Butter...Jelly" waiting transition

a plastic cookie -used for
"Who Took The Cookie From The Cookie Jar"
(We don't steal in our classroom!) dismissal or waiting

Chicka, Chicka

Hello Lysa! You're a real cool cat.
You've got a lot of this and a lot of that!
We all think you are really neat
So come on down and do the Chicka, Chicka beat!

Hands up! Chicka–Chicka, Chicka–Chicka; *(raise hands up)*
Hands down! Chicka–Chicka, Chicka–Chicka; *(lower hands down)*
To the left – Chicka–Chicka, Chicka–Chicka; *(slide to the left)*
To the right – Chicka–Chicka, Chicka–Chicka; *(slide to the right)*
To the top – Chicka–Chicka, Chicka–Chicka; *(lift arms above head)*
To the bottom – Chicka–Chicka, Chicka–Chicka. *(lower arms to feet)*

The Hello Song

Hello, hello, hello and how are you?
I'm fine, I'm fine
and I hope that you are, too.

Hola, hola, ¿hola como estas tu?
Estoy bien, estoy bien
Y espero tu tambien.

©Karen's Kids

Teacher Talk

The following transition, **Lotion Commotion,** is very effective to use with young children when you are waiting for them to gather for a large group experience. Their little hands are busy, and it is a wonderful sensory experience!

**Brenda Bowline – Pre-K II
SFA Lab School**

Lotion Commotion

Teacher says: "There's a lotion commotion going through the ocean."

(Repeat the phrase as you give each child some lotion to rub on their hands. Some children will rub the lotion all over themselves! It is very soothing and occupies them as they are waiting for their friends to gather before a group time.)

Variations: Try using different scents, but be aware of any skin allergies the children in your classroom may have. Choose a lotion that is safe to use with young children.

Clap Your Hands

Clap you hands, clap your hands, clap them just like me.
Touch your shoulders, touch your shoulders, touch them just like me.
Tap your knees, tap your knees, tap them just like me.
Shake your head, shake your head, shake it just like me.
Clap your hands, clap your hands, now let them quiet be.

Story Starters

The teacher begins a story.
Children are called to add a sentence to the story.

Teacher Talk

Little Sally Walker works well to draw children into the group. My children love this and will clean up fast to get to the rug. It also works well to get their wiggles out before a small or large group time. Clap your hands and do it with the children. It gets the children up and moving around so they will be ready to settle down and listen.

Tammy Wall - Pre-K I
SFA Lab School

Little Sally Walker

Little Sally Walker walking down the street.
She didn't have anything to do so she walked in front of you.
She said, "Hey girls do your dance, do your dance then STOP!
        Hey girls do your dance, do your dance then STOP!
        Hey girls do your dance, do your dance then STOP
(girls stand up and do their dance)
Now FREEZE and slowly melt down.
(girls FREEZE and melt down to the floor in a sitting position)

Variations: Repeat using boys, pre-k, individual children's names, colors they are wearing, hair length, types of clothes, etc.

Do as I'm Doing, Follow, Follow Me

Do as I'm doing, follow, follow me.
Do as I'm doing, follow, follow me.

If I do it high (do 'it' up high).
    or low (do 'it' down low).

If I do it fast (do 'it' up fast).
    or slow (do 'it' downs low).

Do as I'm doing, follow, follow me.
Do as I'm doing, follow, follow me.

Father Abraham Had Seven Sons

CHORUS
Father Abraham had seven sons,
Seven sons had Father Abraham.
They didn't laugh—uh, uh!
The didn't cry—oh, no!
All they did was go like this!

1. To the right...*children repeat* To the right! *(stretch and fold right arm)*

CHORUS

2. To the right...to the left *(stretch and fold left arm)*
3. To the right...to the left...shake a right *(shake right foot)*
4. To the right...to the left...shake a right...shake a left *(shake left foot)*
5. To the right...to the left...shake a right...shake a left...turn around
   (turn around)
6. To the right...to the left...shake a right...shake a left...turn around...nod
   your head *(nod your head)*

ENDING: All they did was sit right down! *(sit down)*

Finger Plays and Nursery Rhymes

One child says the first line of a finger play, nursery rhyme, or short poem. Children in turn say the next line. While some of the children are participating in the rhymes, other children are being called to use the restroom, get their jackets, etc.

Head and Shoulders
(To the tune of Mary Had a Little Lamb)

Eyes and ears and mouths and nose.
Head and shoulders, knees and toes;
Knees and toes, knees and toes.
Head and shoulders, knees and toes;

Head Shoulders Baby!

Head—shoulders baby
One, two, three

Head—shoulders baby
One, two, three

Head—shoulders, head—shoulders, head—shoulders baby
One, two, three

Shoulders—tummy baby (the repeat pattern)
Tummy—knees baby (the repeat pattern)
Knees—feet baby (the repeat pattern)

Repeat backwards
Feet—knees baby until you get back to Shoulders—head baby. The last verse is "Sit down baby, one, two three; sit down baby, one, two, three. Sit down. Sit down. Sit down baby, one, two, three.

Helicopter Ride

Tiptoes up.
Tiptoes down.
Start your motor and turn around.
Spread your arms out to your side.
Twist and twist for the helicopter ride.

Teacher Talk

This is a fun and effective transition, **Wiggle Worm,** *that can be used with younger children to get the wiggles out while they are waiting for all of their friends to gather for small or large group experiences. When playing games that children are called on to give answers, you will usually have other children call out the answer, which in turn upsets the child you have called on to answer the question. To diffuse this situation, I look directly at the child I called on and tell him or her that I can only hear his or her words; and then I wait for him or her to give or to repeat the answer. The student always looks at me, amazed I can only hear his words! It's simple, but it works every time!*

Brenda Bowline – Pre-K II
SFA Lab School

Wiggle Worm

Prepare a set of 3" x 5" index cards programmed with lowercase and capital letters. To this set, add six to eight cards that only have a picture of a worm on them. Place the cards in a can with a lid, such as a coffee can. Decorate the can and label it, "Wiggle Worm."

The teacher first calls on a child and then pulls a card out of the can. When you call on a child first, the children understand that only that child is supposed to answer. The child can say the name of the letter or the sound the letter makes. If a worm is pulled out, the child says, "Wiggle Worm!" and all of the children have to wiggle. In addition to being a fun transition, "Wiggle Worm" can be used as an informal assessment tool to find out what your children know about the alphabet, e.g., letter recognition, and letter/sound recognition.

Variations: *Wiggle Worm card can be programmed with numerals.*

How Do/Does Game

How does the horn go?
How do the windshield wipers go?

How does the birdie go?
How do cars go?

Children respond by making the sound and doing the action.

I'm Looking for...

I'm looking for children who...
...have one hand on their head and the
other hand on their foot.

...are sitting on the rug with their hands in their laps.

As a majority of children comply, begin group time.

I Wiggle

I wiggle my fingers.
I wiggle my toes.
I wiggle my shoulder.
I wiggle my nose.
Now no more wiggles are left in me.
So I'll be as still, as still as can be.

Keep the Rhythm

The teacher claps a rhythm and children repeat it.

The teacher can vary this by snapping, stomping, jumping, etc.

Lap, Lap, Clap, Clap, Single Snap, Single Snap

While children are waiting for everyone to come to the rug, everyone claps their lap 2 times together, their hands 2 times together, and each hand snaps separately in order to create a pattern. When the children are snapping, the first snap a child states his/her own name and the second snap he/she states a friend's name. Then it's the friend's turn.

Little Sir Echo

Little Sir Echo-o how do you do?
Hel-lo, (hel-lo), hel-lo, (hel-lo).
Little Sir Ech-o I'm calling you,
Hel-lo, (hel-lo)! Hel-lo, (hel-lo)!
Hel-lo, (hel-lo)! Hel-lo, (hel-lo)
Won't you come over and play? (and play!)
You're a nice little fellow I know by your voice
But you're always so far away (away!)

Looking Through the Window
(use a large picture frame without the glass)

The teacher looks through the window and sings to the tune of "Go in and out the Window"

I'm looking through the window,
I'm looking through the window,
I'm looking through the window,
To see someone I love.

Teacher chooses a child and continues.

Mr. Edd, Edd, Edd

Oh Mr. Edd, Edd, Edd
Got out of bed, bed, bed
And he bumped his head, head, head
On a piece of cornbread, bread, bread.

Edd called for the doctor, doctor, doctor *(dial a phone)*
And the doctor said, said, said, *(point finger and shake)*
"Get up EDD! You're not dead! All you got was a bump on the head."

Edd got up and went upon the hill. *(climbing motion, swing arms)*
He started shaking like an automobile. *(shake)*
To the front, *(jump to the front)*
To the back; *(jump to the back)*
To the side-side-side! *(jump from side-to-side)*

To the front, *(jump to the front)*
To the back; *(jump to the back)*
Now sit down, down, down! *(sit down)*

Punchinello

Hey Punchinello, Punchinello funny fellow.
Hey Punchinello, Punchinello funny you.

What can you do Punchinello, Punchinello funny fellow?
What can you do Punchinello, Punchinello funny you?

We can do it too, Punchinello funny fellow.
We can do it too, Punchinello funny you!!

Oh Mother, Mother May I?

Oh, mother, mother may I? May I? May I?
Oh, mother, mother may I? Play this game with you.
Take one step (step forward)
Take one step (step forward)
Oh, mother, mother may I, Play this game with you?

Variations: scissor steps, baby steps, bunny steps

One, Two, Three, Four, Five

1-2-3-4-5 on one hand.
1-2-3-4-5 on the other hand.
Five on one hand.
Five on the other hand.
Five and five make TEN!

My Hands Upon My Head I Place

My hands upon my head I place,
On my shoulders, on my face.
Now I raise them up so high
And make my fingers fairly fly.
Now I clap the, one, two, three
Then I fold them silently.

Name That Tune

The teacher hums or plays a familiar tune.
Children try to name the song.

Ronald McDonald—a Biscuit

Ronald McDonald—a biscuit
Ronald McDonald—a biscuit

A shoe, shoe,wa-wa
A shoe, shoe,wa-wa

Down, down baby
Down by the roller coaster

Sweet, sweet baby
Down by the roller coaster

Shimmy-shimmy cocoa-pop
Shimmy-shimmy POW!
Shimmy-shimmy cocoa-pop
Shimmy-shimmy POW!

Sensory Words

The teacher says a word then asks children what the word makes them think of or how it makes them feel. This is a wonderful way to expand children's vocabularies.

sunny	pebbly	moist	cluck
muddy	gobble	sweet	playful
merry	scared	gloomy	excite

Two Little Hands

Two little hands go clap, clap, clap.
Two little feet go tap, tap, tap.
One little body turns around.
One little body sits quietly down.

The Ants Go Marching

The ants go marching one-by-one. Hooray! Hooray!
The ants go marching one-by-one. Hooray! Hooray!
The ants go marching one-by-one,
The little one stops to suck his thumb,
And they all go marching, down…into the ground…to get out…of the rain.
Boom! Boom! Boom!!

two---tie his shoe
three—climb a tree
four—to shut the door
five—to rob the hive
six—to pick up sticks
seven—to look up at heaven
eight—to shut the gate
nine—to stop and dine
ten—to say, "The End!"

Beans, Beans, Beans

Beans, Beans, Beans
Baked beans, butter beans
Big, fat lima beans,
Long, thin string beans-
Those are just a few.

Green beans, black beans,
Big, fat kidney beans,
Red, hot chili beans,
Jumping beans, too.

Pea beans, pinto beans,
Don't forget 'shelly' beans.

Last of all, best of all,
I like jelly beans!

Once Upon a Time in a Nursery Rhyme

Once upon a time in a nursery rhyme, there were three bears.
One was the PaPa Bear *(say this in a low, gruff voice)*.
One was the MaMa Bear *(say this in a medium, soft voice)*.
And one was the weee—Little Bear *(say in a high-pitched, shrill voice)*.

They all went a walkin' in the deep woods a talkin'
When along came a little girl with long, flowing golden curls.
Her name was Goldilocks. Up on the door she knocks.
No one was there...she didn't care.
She walked right in and had herself a ball.
She didn't care, no one was there.

Home came the three bears.
"Someone's been eating my por-ridge!" said the Papa Bear, said the Papa Bear.
"Someone's been eating my por-ridge!" sat the MaMa Bear, said the MaMa Bear.
"Hey! Momma-ree bear!" said the Little Weee-Bear,
"Someone's broken my chair! HEY!!"

Goldilocks woke up, and broke up the party, and beat it out of there.
"Bye, bye, bye, bye, bye!" said the PaPa Bear, said the PaPa Bear.
"Bye, bye, bye, bye, bye!" said the MaMa Bear, said the MaMa Bear.
"Hey! Momma-ree bear!" said the Little Weee-Bear,
"Someone's broken my chair! HEY!!

Teacher Talk

Teacher Talk

*I use **I am Waiting** when I am waiting for just a few friends to get to the rug. The children love to sing along with me and it keeps them engaged while waiting for everyone to get on the rug. You can add different things for the children to do at the end.*

Lynsey McAninch 2nd Grade
SFA Charter School
SFASU 2008 and 2011

I am Waiting

I am waiting, I am waiting,
Just for you, just for you,
Show me that you're ready,
Show me that you're ready,
1, 2, 3, -- eyes on me!
1, 2, 3, -- smiling at me!
1, 2, 3, -- listening to me!

Three-Dimensional Shape Hunt

On the chalkboard, write the name of a shape and draw a 3-D shape. Have children look around the room and name objects that are the same shape. Encourage children to name other things they have seen that are the same shape.

cylinder – pointer, straw, tin can, etc

cube – box, die, sugar cube, etc

cone - ice cream cone, block, etc

sphere – globe, doorknob, ball, grape, marble, etc

True-False

Make a number of true and false statements. IF the answer is true, children pat their knees. If the answer is false, children sit still.

Birds fly.
Dogs meow.
Babies growl.
Sun rains.
Apples are white.
Tables swim.

ADD YOUR OWN.

©Karen's Kids

Two Little Black Birds

Two little blackbirds sitting on the hill.
One named Jack and the other named Jill.
Fly away Jack. Fly away Jill.
Come back Jack. Come back Jill.

Two little blackbirds sitting on the wall.
One named Peter and the other named Paul.
Fly away Peter. Fly away Paul.
Come back Peter. Come back Paul.

We are Waiting for Three Friends
(To the tune of Johnny Works with One Hammer)

We are waiting for three friends, three friends, three friends,
We are waiting for three friends to join us on the rug.

We are waiting for Allison, Allison, Allison,
We are waiting for Allison to join us on the rug.

Teacher Talk

Waddleeeachah is great for waiting or even getting attention. The older students enjoy it when you get faster and faster each time. REMEMBER to slow down the last time you plan on singing it so the children will begin to calm down! In this song or chant you are also CROSSING THE MIDPOINT of our body…which is helping the "brain to grow."

Cay McAninch
Elementary Education Department
SFASU 1978 and 1982

Waddleeeachah

(pat)   (pat)   (clap)(clap)   (hands over)   (hands over)
Waddle - ee - acha   - Waddle - ee - acha

(nose/shoulder)   (nose/shoulder)   (wave/elbow)   (wave/elbow)
A—doodle   - ee-doo   - A- doodle   - ee-doo

(repeat)

(pat)   (pat)   (clap)   (clap)   (hands over)   (hands over)
Simplest   thing   there   isn't much   to it.

(nose/shoulder)   (nose/shoulder)   (wave/elbow)   (wave/elbow)
All you've have to   do is   doddle-ee   -   doo it.

(pat)   (pat) (clap)   (clap)   (hands over) (hands over)
I   like   the   rest of it,   but what I   like best is…

(nose)   (shoulder)   (nose)   (shoulder)
the doodle   - ee   - doodle   -   ee

(nose)   (shoulder)   (nose)   (shoulder)
doodle -   ee   - doodle -   ee

(nose)   (shoulder) (nose)   (shoulder)
doodle -   ee   - doodle -   e – do ------

YEAH!

Who Stole the Cookie from the Cookie Jar?

Class: Who stole the cookie from the cookie jar?

Sarah stole the cookie from the cookie jar!

Sarah: Who me?

Class: Yes you!!

Sarah: Couldn't be.

Class: Then who?

Sarah: Emily stole the cookie from the cookie jar.

Where is Thumbkin?

Where is Thumbkin? Where is Thumbkin?
Here I am. Here I am.
How are you today, sir?
Very well, I thank you.
Run away! Run away!

Substitute:
Pointer
Tall Man or Middle Man
Ring Man
Pinky

©KGF

Herman the Worm

Sitting on the fence post,
Chewing my bubble gum.
(chomp-chomp, chomp-chomp)
Playing with my yo-yo.
(wheeoo, wheeoo)
Along came Herman the worm.
He was -----this big.
I said, "Herman, what happened?"
⠀⠀⠀⠀"I ate my sister!"
I said, "Herman, don't eat your family.
Sitting on the fence post,
Chewing my bubble gum.
(chomp-chomp, chomp-chomp)
Playing with my yo-yo.
(wheeoo, wheeoo)
Along came Herman the worm.
He was ---------------this big.
I said, "Herman, what happened?"
⠀⠀⠀"I ate my brother!"
I said, "Herman, don't eat your family.
Sitting on the fence post,
Chewing my bubble gum.
(chomp-chomp, chomp-chomp)
Playing with my yo-yo.
(wheeoo, wheeoo)
Along came Herman the worm.
He was ----------------------this big.
I said, "Herman, what happened?"
⠀⠀⠀"I ate my mama!"
I said," Herman, don't eat your family!"
Sitting on the fence post,
Chewing my bubble gum.
(chomp-chomp, chomp-chomp)
Playing with my yo-yo.
(wheeoo, wheeoo)
Along came Herman the worm.
He was ----------------------------------this big.
I said, "Herman, what happened?"
⠀⠀⠀"I ate my daddy!"
I said, "Herman, don't eat your family
Sitting on the fence post,
Chewing my bubble gum.
(chomp-chomp, chomp-chomp)
Playing with my yo-yo.
(wheeoo-wheeoo)
along came Herman the worm.
He was ------ this big!
I said, "Herman, what happened? **"I BURPED!"**

This is a great way to introduce measurement to young children.

You may substitute vegetables, fruits, bugs, animals that gradually get larger each time...in place of family members.

Teacher Talk

This **Thank You** transition is great for positive reinforcement for those who have done what you have asked. It may be a follow-up transition as children are coming to the rug after a clean up time. It is amazing how quiet children will become to receive the positive reinforcement!

Lauree Hayes – 3rd grade
SFA Charter School
SFASU 1982 and 1988

Thank You
(To the tune of *Frere Jacques*)

Thank you, _____.
Thank you, _____.
Thank you, _____.
Thank you, _____.
Thank you, _____.

Variations: When a child (or children) are "dragging their feet" a little bit, you can use the "almost thank you" in place of "thank you" following with "thanks you" when the desired behavior has occurred.

Little Bunny Rabbit
(To the tune of *Battle Hymn of Republic*)

Little bunny rabbit had a fly upon his nose.
Little bunny rabbit had a fly upon his nose.
Little bunny rabbit had a fly upon his nose.

And he ... flicked it and it flew away!

Little bunny rabbit had a fly upon his nose... on his ____.
Little bunny rabbit had a fly upon his nose... on his ____.
Little bunny rabbit had a fly upon his nose... on his ____.

And he flicked it and it flew away.

(Repeat and add upon his nose, on his ___, on his ____, etc.

What's That You Say?

Start in a circle with your arms around each other's shoulders. Everyone begins to march with their heads down. The person giving the instructions raises up and says,

"Let me see your Frankenstein!"
and the kids pop up their heads and say
"What's that you say?"

"Let me see your Frankenstein!"
and the kids pop up their heads and say
"What's that you say?"

"Let me see your Frankenstein!"
and the kids pop up their heads and say
"What's that you say?"

(motions – act like Frankenstein and say...)

"Um Bopa, Um Bopa, Um Bopa , BOW BOW"
"Um Bopa, Um Bopa, Um Bopa , BOW BOW"

Repeat using substitutions for <u>Frankenstein</u>...such as...

*wiggle worm *cry baby *muscle man *dinosaur *twirlly birds*
*jumping jacks *baby kicks *jelly legs *funky chicken

Roll Call Thinking

Waiting/Dismissal Transitions

Have the children answer the question to call roll or use as a transition instead of saying "here."

...your last name

...your favorite smell

...something red

...something hard

...name of a President

...an animal that lives in the ocean

...something made of wood

...something oval shaped

...favorite book to read

...last present you opened

... # of family members living in your house

...number greater than _____

...something that attracts to a magnet

...a three syllable word

...a word that rhymes with _____

...something that is green and long

...something that is soft, red, and big

You will discover the children will help you think of things at "thinking" time.

Teacher Talk

Often times I taught my students a traditional song or chant like **No More Pie** *by Ella Jenkins. Once the tune or beat was established, I changed the words to meet the needs of the students and the situation.*

Carolyn Davis
Elementary Education Department
SFASU 1977 and 1982

No More Pie
by Ella Jenkins
Original Echo Chant:

Oh my, (students echo)
I want a piece of pie. (students echo)
The pie's too sweet. (students echo)
I want a piece of meat. (students echo)
The meat's too red. (students echo)
I want a piece of bread. (students echo)
The bread's too brown. (students echo)
I'll have to go to town. (students echo)
Town's too far. (students echo)
I'll have to take my car. (students echo)
The car's too slow. (students echo)
I fell and stumped my toe. (students echo)
My toe's got a pain. (students echo)
I better take the train. (students echo)
The train had a wreck. (students echo)
I nearly broke my neck. (students echo)
Oh my, (students echo)
I WANT A PIECE OF PIE!
Changed version:
Oh my, (students echo)
It's time for writing, (students echo)
I need to get my journal, (students echo)
Get them quietly, (students echo)
Pencils are necessary, (students echo)
It's time to _____ ...
(whatever you want them to do), (students echo)

Not Last Night but the Night Before

Not last night, but the night before	JUMP BACK, BABY! JUMP BACK
I saw 24 robbers at my back door	JUMP BACK, BABY! JUMP BACK
Well, I go up to let 'em in.	JUMP BACK, BABY! JUMP BACK
And I hit 'em over the head with a fryin' pan.	JUMP BACK, BABY! JUMP BACK
Well, one flew east and one flew west.	JUMP BACK, BABY! JUMP BACK
And one flew over the cukoo's nest.	JUMP BACK, BABY! JUMP BACK!

I said, "Flee!" "FLEE!!"
"Flee – fly." "FLEE – FLY."

"Flee – Fly – Flow." "FLEE! FLY! FLOW!"
"Vista." "VISTA!"
"Cume lada." "CUME LADA!"
"Cumelada, cumelada, cume la vista!"
(repeat)
"Oh, no, no, no not a vista. Oh, no, no, no, not a vee!
"Eenie-meenie esa-meenie"
"Ooo-wada, wada-meenie"
"Esa-meenie, sala-meenie"
"Ooo-wadeh, Waah!"
"Beep-diddily, oaten doaten"
"Bee-bop-ska-deeten, dahten"
"SHHHHHHHHH!" "VISTA!" (shout)

The Princess Pat
The teacher sings,
and the children ECHO.
Actions may be made up
to go with words.

The Princess Pat,	ECHO
Lived in a tree.	ECHO
She sailed across	ECHO
The Seven Seas.	ECHO
She sailed across	ECHO
The channel, too.	ECHO
And brought with her,	ECHO
A rig of bamboo.	ECHO
A rig of bamboo!	ECHO
Now, what is that?	ECHO
It's something made	ECHO
By the Princess Pat.	ECHO
It's red and gold	ECHO
And purple, too!	ECHO
That's why it's called	ECHO
A rig of bamboo.	ECHO
Now, Captain Jack	ECHO
Had a mighty fine crew.	ECHO
They sailed across	ECHO
The channel, too.	ECHO
But their ship sank,	ECHO
And your's will, too.	ECHO
If you don't take	ECHO
A rig of bamboo!	ECHO
A rig of bamboo!	ECHO
Now, what is that?	ECHO
It's something made	ECHO
By the Princess Pat.	ECHO
It's red and gold	ECHO
And purple, too!	ECHO
That's why it's called	ECHO
A rig of bamboo.	ECHO

Shortnin' Bread

CHORUS:
Momma's little baby loves shortnin', shortnin';
Momma's little baby loves shortnin' bread.

Get out the skillet! Get out the lid!
Momma's gonna make a little shortnin' bread.
That ain't all, she's a-gonna do!
Momma's gonna make a little coffee, too.

Momma's little baby loves shortnin', shortnin';
Momma's little baby loves shortnin' bread.

Two little children, a-lying in the bed.
One most sick and the other most dead.
Called for the doctor and the doctor said,
"Give those children some shortnin' bread!"

Momma's little baby loves shortnin', shortnin';
Momma's little baby loves shortnin' bread.

Two more children, jumpin' on the bed.
One fell off and bumped his head.
Called for the doctor and the doctor sad,
"Get up ED! You're not dead! All you got was a bump on the head."

Ed got up and went upon the hill.
He started shaking like an automobile.

(Do the actions)
To the front, to the back; to the side-side-side!
To the front, to the back; now sit down, down, down!

Teacher Talk

*I LOVE to entertain. Yes, I am a superstar in my classroom, and I love to get down with **Wiggle it...just a little bit ;)** A few years ago there was a little plush cheerleader doll that sang a cute little diddy, and I started to use it in the classroom to help my third-graders stretch on a test day.*

Jessica Jones
Raguet Elementary
SFASU 2006

Wiggle it...just a little bit ;)

I stomp my feet
I boogie to the beat
I turn around and touch the ground
And then I wiggle it, just a little bit
(I usually add some fist pumps here)
(teacher prompts students to try it a little faster)
Repeat the verse and get faster
Then slower

Repeat the verse until you are in slow, robot mode.

A-ram, Sam, Sam

A ram, sam, sam
A ram, sam, sam
Gooley, gooley,
gooley, gooley, gooley
Ram, sam, sam

A-raffi, A-raffi,
Gooley, gooley,
gooley, gooley,
Ram, sam, sam

Teacher Talk

This is What I Can Do *is a great game for wait time. The teacher begins and then each child gets a turn until everybody is at the rug. After some practice, it is a great silent transition going down the hallway. Just have it go straight down the line with each student getting a turn until you reach your destination. It keeps hands busy and voices silent!*

Lindsey Burns – 2st Grade
R.V. Groves Elementary - Wylie, TX
SFASU 2009

This is What I Can Do

This is what I can do; see if you can do it to. (doing and action with body)
This is what I can do; now I pass it on to ____. (child's name)

This is what _____ (child chosen) can do; see if you can do it to.
This is what _____ (child's name) can do; now you pass it on to who?
(child chooses a friend)

What Goes With It?

The child learns that one object is dependent upon the use of another. Substitute pictures if real objects are unavailable.

A knife goes with a _____.(fork)

hammer	nail
mitten	hand
chair	table
salt	pepper
shoe	foot
hat	head
key	lock
bread	butter

Moving

Movement is natural for children. Many students in our classrooms are kinesthetic learners and need to move often. Movement transitions are a GREAT opportunity for reviewing new or old content while encouraging appropriate movement within the classroom.

Teacher Talk:

*As classroom teachers, we seem to spend a good deal of time traveling with our students. We go as a group to music, lunch, and PE. We also find ourselves waiting until it's our turn to enter the next class. The **Alphabet Walk** is a great way to keep minds focused and productive while moving and waiting. If your school demands that you move and wait quietly, you can always use a whisper voice to do the Alphabet Walk or take the opportunity to learn and practice the American Sign Language manual alphabet.*

Paula Griffin – SFASU
Elementary Education Department
SFASU 1978-1983

The Alphabet Walk

As you are moving your class from place to place or waiting your turn, work on the alphabet.
Teacher begins by saying, "A".
Students respond, "B".

This sequence continues to the end of the alphabet.
You can vary it by giving students the lead or dividing them into groups (male and female, etc.) or vary the sequence such as
Teacher says, "A, B".
Students respond, "C, D".

This also works well with rote counting, skip counting, or counting by 5's and 10's.

Teacher Talk

*This transition, **Show Me**, is one of our favorites. It gets them ready to move through the hall without disturbing other classes.*

Cathy May – Kindergarten
Shawnee Trail Elementary, Frisco
SFASU 2001

Show Me
(To the tune of The More We Get Together)

Show me what your hands do, your hands do, your hands do.
Show me what your hands do when you stand in line.
Show me what you mouth does...
Show me what your feet do...

Move Like

Move like a _____,
(bee, bird, elephant, snake,
bug, frog, dog, cat, etc.)

 to the _____
(restroom, table, line, etc.)

The following transition, **Have a Seat,** is a great way to bring the whole group to the rug following an activity or learning centers. The teacher begins the chant, and the kids join in as they are coming to the rug. It can be repeated until everyone is seated and ready.

Becky Griffith – 2nd Grade
SFA Charter School
SFASU 1984 and 1986

Have a Seat!

Have a seat!
(clap)
Have a seat!
(clap)
Take a load off your feet!
(clap, clap)

You Put One Hand on the Rail
(To the tune of *Farmer in the Dell*)

You put one hand on the rail…
The other on your head.
You take a step,
And take a step,
And give a little twist.

©KGF

Can You Walk?

Can you walk, can you walk? Can you walk along?
Can you sing, can you sing? Can you sing this song?

Can you walk, can you walk? Can you plant a pose?
Freeze now! Head to toes.

Variation:
change walk to skate, slide, slither, tiptoe, etc.

Follow the Leader

As you lead the line, walk in patterns or move your arms to keep the followers challenged to pay attention.

Walk-a-Roni
(To the tune of Yankee Doodle)

Yankee Doodle went to town
A riding on a pony
Stuck a feather in his hat
And called it _____-a-roni

In the blank, use action words:
walk, jog, skip, sneak, etc.

Trot Old Joe

Trot Old Joe, Trot Old Joe
You trot better'n any horse I know.
Trot Old Joe, Trot Old Joe
You're the best horse in the country-o
WHOA! Joe!

Variations:
Replace trot with walk, skip, jog, run, etc.

Tour Rope

Place knots about every two feet in a long rope.
Children hold the knot as they walk.

The Little Tiny Man
(To the tune of Jimmy Crack Corn)

The little tiny man takes little tiny steps.
Oh, the little tiny man takes little tiny steps.
The little tiny man takes little tiny steps.
He claps and he turns around.

The little tiny man takes little tiny steps.

Variation:
The great big man takes great big steps.
The funny crooked man takes funny crooked steps.
The backwards man takes backwards steps.

The Thousand Legged Worm

Oh, the thousand legged worm
As she began to squirm
Said, "Has anybody seen a leg of mine?
If it can't be found, I'll just have to hop around
On the other nine hundred, ninety-nine!"

Hop around, HOP! HOP!
Hop around, HOP! HOP
On the other nine hundred, ninety-nine.
"If it can't be found, I'll just have to hop around
On the other nine hundred, ninety-nine"

Make a large circle out of a full sheet of poster board. Cut out two large eyes. Add antennae using pipe cleaners and Styrofoam balls. The "head" of the worm holds the "face" for one verse as children move. At the end of the verse, the "head" is passed to the next child in line and the first "head" becomes the caboose of the worm.

Teacher Talk

The following transition, **Hoochi Coochie,** *can be used when you need to move children from sitting to standing or standing to sitting. It is fun, quick, and very eff...*

Brenda Bowline – Pre-K II
SFA Lab School

Hoochi Coochie

Teacher says – "1, 2, 3, 4 hoochie coochie off the floor."
or
Teacher says – "1, 2, 3, 4 hoochie coochie to the floor."

Variations: Count in Spanish

Oh, You Walk and You Walk

Oh, you walk, and you walk, and you walk, and you STOP!
You walk, and you walk, and you walk, and you STOP!
You walk, and you walk, and you walk, and you STOP!
You walk, and you walk, and you stop.

Variation: Change walk to other movements:

jump, hop, skate, slide, sneak, wiggle, bounce, etc.

Teacher Talk

Ready for the Hall *was actually shared in one of my classes by a former intern. It is a great transition for reminding children what they need to do to get ready to leave the room and travel down the hall. It helps them to focus on appropriate behavior while moving from place to place.*

Jannah Nerren
Elementary Education Department
SFASU

Ready for the Hall

My hands are hanging at my sides
I'm standing straight and tall
My eyes are looking straight ahead
I'm ready for the hall!

Variations: At one of my schools, children are required to hold their hands behind their backs when moving in the hall. They call this "Tigers in their den." So a variation on the transition to fit this need is:

My tiger is tucked in his den
I'm standing straight and tall
My eyes are looking straight ahead
I'm ready for the hall!

Oh, Mother, Mother May I?

Oh, Mother, Mother may I, may I, may I
Oh, Mother, Mother may I play this game with you?

Take one step...
Take two steps...
Take one step...
Take two steps...

Oh, Mother, Mother may I play this game with you?

Teacher Talk

*The following transition, **Radio**, was one I used when my kindergarten class was walking to lunch which was far and we had to stay in a line. I found that if I would keep them busy I had less behavior problems with pushing, shoving, and running!*

Cay McAninch
Elementary Education Department
SFASU 1978 and 1982

Radio

When walking in a line with teacher leading...

Teacher: "Turn your radios on – sound like a dinosaur."
Students: Make dinosaur sounds of their choice.
Teacher: Put hand in the air and say, "Change the channel. Sound like a cat."
Students: Make cat sounds.

When it is time to be quiet to enter a building...
Teacher: "Turn you radios off"
Students: Students switch to off and swallow their sounds.

Variations: Think of any animal sounds, they can walk like a ____, they can become a helicopter, etc.

Do As I'm Doing

Do as I'm doing, follow, follow me.
Do as I'm doing, follow, follow me.
I can do it high or low.
I can do it fast or slow.
Do as I'm doing, follow, follow me.

(Fill in the "I" with other children's names and let them lead something.)

Clean UP

©KGF

Cleaning up and shifting from one activity to another is difficult for children of all ages. With the use of transitions, movement into another part of the day can be accomplished with ease by using engaging activities.

Teacher Talk

Making clean up "fun" is important in gaining support from our little and big ones. I have used this song with all ages!

Lori Harkness - SFASU
Director of SFA Lab School
SFASU 1995-1998

Clean It UP
(To the tune of the *Adam's Family*)

Clean it up (snap, snap)
Clean it up (snap, snap)
Clean it up, Clean it up, Clean it up (snap, snap)

Variations: I have also used this transition to "line it up", "move it on", and "sit right down".

I Can Help Now
(To the tune of *Are You Sleeping*)

I can help now.
I can help now.
Clean the center.
Clean the center.
I can put the things away.
I can put the things away.
Nicely and neatly.
Nicely and neatly.

©Karen's Kids

I Clean Up

Pick it Up!

Pick, pick, pick it;
pick it up, pick it up.
Pick, pick, pick it;
pick it up, pick it up.
Pick, pick, pick it;
pick it up, pick it up.
Pick, pick, pick it;
pick it up, pick it up.

©KGF

Counting and Clean-Up

Have each child pick up TWO items and put them away. This is particularly effective for picking up small pieces or toys. Change the number of items you want children to pick up.

Will You Clean-up?
(To the tune of *Lazy Mary*)

Drew and Steve will you clean up?
Will you clean up?
Will you clean up?
Drew and Steve will you clean up?
And make the centers clean?

Oh, Do You Know What Time it Is?
(To the tune of *Mulberry Bush*)

Oh, do you know what time it is? What time it is? What time it is?
Oh, do you know what time it is? It's time to clean up now.

Playing Music

Teacher Talk

*Carolyn Davis introduced me to my favorite way to 'clean up' young children and prepare them to move into the next activity of the day. The children knew when they heard the **Good Morning** song on the Greg and Steve CD it was time to clean up centers and go to the rug for our opening activities. Later in the day, after literacy centers, when they heard the Jack Hartmann CD **Rhymin' to the Beat,** they new it was time for Rhyme Time (playing with nursery rhymes). In the afternoon after a reading time, they knew when they heard the **Math in Motion** CD by Jack Hartmann it was time for Math Stations."*

Not only did playing this music allow me to signal to the children my expectations it allowed me to help them clean up. Since many of the songs on the CDs were familiar to the children when they were waiting on the rug they were kept occupied by singing and moving to the music. This way of cleaning up was a LIFESAVER for me and extremely effective with young or older children.

**Cay McAninch – SFASU
Elementary Education Department
SFASU 1978 and 1982**

Some of my favorites CDs are:

Kids in Action	Greg and Steve
Kids in Motion	Greg and Steve
Dr. Jean and Friends	Jean Feldman
Fundamentals	CJ (Shirley Handy)
Listen	CJ (Shirley Handy)
Hip Hop Alpha Bop	Jack Hartmann
Shake, Rattle, and Read	Jack Hartmann
Math in Motion	Jack Hartmann
Math Alll Around Me	Jack Hartmann
Rhymin to the Beat-1	Jack Hartmann
Everything Grows	Raffi

Clean-Up

Hickory-Dickory Dock

Hickory Dickory Dock

Time has run out on the clock

The clock says now

To clean our room

Hickory Dickory Dock

Tick-tock!

We're Cleaning up our Room
(To the tune of *Farmer in the Dell*)

We're cleaning up our room.
We're cleaning up our room.
We're putting all our things away.
We're cleaning up our room.

©*KGF*

Traditional Clean Up Song

Clean up! Clean up! Everybody do your share.
Clean up! Clean up! Everybody everywhere.

Make your centers nice and neat. Make them really clean.
Every body clean up, clean up, clean up.
Everybody clean up, clean up now.

Teaching

With the correct choices, transitions are an invaluable tool in the classroom of older elementary students as well as younger children. Use transition times to review math, science, spelling, etc. The possibilities are unlimited.

Teacher Talk

This transition works well for waiting times because you can sing as many verses as you need by substituting different number sets from 0-5. This transition engages children in oral language, fine motor, and numeracy skills while waiting for everyone to gather.

Liz Vaughan – Pre-K
SFASU 1974 and 1977

The Adding Song
(To to the tune of *Skip to My Lou*)

Give me a 2; let's have a set of 2.
(Hold up 2 fingers on one hand.)
Give me a 3.; let's have a set of 3.
(Hold up 3 fingers on the other hand.)
Put them together; add the 2 and 3,
(Put hands together.)
And you'll have a set of____.
(Allow children to call out answer.)

Repeat inserting different number sets from 0-5.

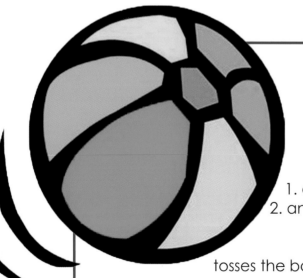

Beach Ball Questions

The teacher throws a beach ball to a child. The child catching the beach ball does one of two things:

1. answer a question on the beach ball
2. answer the question the teacher poses

The child with the beach ball either tosses the ball to a friend or back to the teacher.

Questions can come from any content area.

Teacher Talk

This song and transition activity is a great way to reinforce content understanding after a study of the planets. The teacher needs picture cards for each of the planets. The group engage together singing the song and then dismiss by identifying the planet picture card and identifying one characteristic of the planet. Each planet is repeated ensuring multiple characteristics are addressed and all students are dismissed.

Erica S. Dillard, Instructor
SFASU 1996 & 2001

The Family of the Sun
(To the tune of *Famer in the Dell*)

The family of the Sun, The family of the Sun, There are eight planets in the family of the Sun.

Mercury is hot, And Mercury is small. Mercury has no atmosphere. It's just a rocky ball.

Venus has thick clouds that hide what is below. The air is foul. The ground is hot. It rotates very slow.

We love the Earth our home, its oceans and its trees. We eat its food. We breathe its air. So no pollution, please.

Mars is very red. It's also dry and cold. Some day you might visit Mars if you are really bold.

Great Jupiter is big. We've studied it a lot. We found that it has lots of moons, And a big, red spot.

Saturn has great rings. We wondered what they were. Now we know they're icy rocks. Which we saw as a blur.

Uranus is far. It's cold and greenish-blue. We found it rotates sideways, And it has a lot of moons.

Neptune has a spot. A stormy patch of blue. The planet has a lot of clouds and rings around it, too.

Original Author Unknown; Modified: Dillard (2010)

If You Are Listening

If you are listening, touch your _____.

body parts: Spanish – cabeza, umbros, boca, dientes, nariz, orejas, ojos, pello, etc. OR higher level words – spine, temple, calf, instep, etc.) AVOID the obvious—head, eyes, toes, etc.

If you are listening, clap _____ times.

clapping: Spanish - uno, dos, tres, quatro, etc.

If you are listening, spell _____.

spelling words: practice spelling words for the week

Be creative and make up your own or let the children.

Opposite Song
(To the tune of *Clementine*)

This is UP, this is DOWN, (stand up and squat down)
This is UP, this is DOWN, (stand up and squat down)
This is UP, this is DOWN, (stand up and squat down)
This is UP, this is DOWN. (stand up and squat down)

Variations:
High/low (use arm to indicate high and down low to floor)
Loud/soft (BIG voice on Loud, SOFT voice on Soft)
Fast/slow (roll fists over each other in fast & slow motion)
Big/little (hands & arms out wide, then in very small)
Open/close (use mouth or hands for open/closed)
Awake/asleep (end with asleep and children are quiet)

©'00 Karen D. Handlain

Alice the Camel
(Children called may leave the rug.)

(Fill in each child's name and he/she supplies the next number in the skip counting pattern. Ex: odd, even, 3s, 4s, 5s)

Lauree the camel has 3 humps
Becky the camel has 6 humps
Jan the camel has 9 humps
So go, camels, go! Boom, boom, boom!

***A dismissal transition should be a fast assessment/review
related to the skill, strategy, or procedure
from the lesson when at all possible.***

T-E-X-A-S
(To to the tune of *BINGO*)

We live in a state that we think is great and Texas is its name-O.

T-E-X-A-S
T-E-X-A-S
T-E-X-A-S
And Texas is its name-O.

(REPEAT leaving off one more letter each time repeated, beginning with the **T** and clapping in its place).

Variations: Substitute other words you need to practice.

I Say, You Say

Establish skill pattern (example: +10, +20, -10, -1, -50, rounded to the nearest 10 or 100, Spanish words, phonics, parts of speech, etc).

(Point back and forth from yourself to child, indicating whose turn it is to speak. This can be done with individuals or large groups. Just don't over-kill on this one!)

numbers:	"I say, '34,' you say '44.'"
Teacher:	"34."
Students:	"44."
Teacher:	"34."
Students:	"44."

Spanish words:	"I say, 'Rojo,' you say, 'Red.'"
Teacher:	"Rojo."
Students:	"Red."
Teacher:	"Rojo."
Students:	"Red."

opposites:	"I say, 'Over,' you say, 'Under.'"
Teacher:	"Over."
Students:	"Under."
Teacher:	"Over."
Students:	"Under."

Think of your own!
Also great for an attention getter.

©'00 Karen D Handson

©KGF

L OO PING

Each child is given a card with a number question on it. The first child reads her card.

"I have 2. Who has 2 more than this?"

The child who has the "4" card replies:
"I have 4. Who has 1 less than this?"

The child who as the "3" card replies:
"I have 3. Who has _____ than this?"

Children continue "looping" until the "loop" is complete. Children can be dismissed once they have read their card or the "loop" can be completed.

Name It

©Karen's Kids

(Challenge children to think of something no one else will think of. Use popsicle sticks with one category written on each stick. Pull from the can.)

"Name something you wear on your feet."
"Name something that grows."
"Name something under the ground."
"Name something you can't count."
"Name a vegetable."
(mode of transportation, communication, etc.)

Pass Time
Pass the ball around the circle. Each person relates something he or she learned or enjoyed from that day or week.

Give me an Answer

Popsicle sticks may have children's names on them. During discussions, the teacher pulls a popsicle stick and the child whose name is pulled out answers the question.

Oh, You Walk

Oh, you walk and you walk and you walk and you stop.
You walk and you walk and you walk and you stop.
You walk and you walk and you walk and you stop.
You walk and you walk and you stop.

(Ask the children to replace "walk" with a higher-level movement verb ex: frolic, scamper, lumber, slide, slither.)

Follow the Leader

As you lead the line, walk in **patterns** or move your arms to keep the followers challenged to pay attention.

Counting On

Teacher Says : Counting ON
Teacher Says : 5 – 6 – 7
Students say : 8 – 9 – 10

Variations:
Repeat with number high – low
Sets of 2 – 4
Odd number, even
Use what you are working on in the classroom at the time.

Teacher Talk

Using transitions to review skills can be done at any time. They are a great way to check for understanding and retention of information. The following 8 transitions listed are some of my favorites.

Lysa Hagan – SFASU
SFASU 1987 and 1993

I Say You Say

Establish a number that should be added or subtracted from the number you say for the entire transition of "I say, you say". "Subtract 20 from the number I say." The teacher points at herself, "I say 45," she points at the child, " you say _____." (child should say 25) teacher points at herself, "45" points at child who says, "25", teacher points at herself again, "45", and points at child again who says, "25". The teacher moves to another child to "I say, you say" again. The number you give should vary according to ability of each child. More difficulty may be added or taken away through the number you establish to be added or subtracted, as well as, the number you give to the child. Also, keep in mind that it is easier for children to think forward with adding than backward for subtracting. You may also use multiples "Multiply the number I say by 2."

Word Wall

Use the word wall for many transitions simply by describing a word for the students to guess. Beginning sounds, ending sounds, medial sounds, rhyming words, definitions, number of letters, etc...

Name the Number

"Name the number just before ___." "Name the number just after ___." "Name a number between ___ and ___." "Name an odd number between ___ and ___." "Odd or Even? 23" "Name a number greater than ___." "Name a number less than ____?" "Name a number greater than ___ but less than ____." "Name a multiple of 4."

Telling Time

Have a clock with movable hands. Show a time on the clock with which students should be familiar as you chant to **Oh Do You Know the Muffin Man**:

©KGF

Show a time on the clock, "Can you tell what time it is? (show one child with eye contact on that child). Change the time, "What time it is?" (show a different child). Change the time, "What time it is?" (continue to change the time for each new clock time question while moving from child to child quickly for an answer). Change the time, "Oh do you know what time it is?" change the time, "On my clock?" This continues until all students have had a turn individually or in pairs.

Place Value

After a math lesson on **place value** to the hundreds place, the teacher may ask:

"What is the number in the hundreds place in 364?"
"What is the number in the tens place in 845?"
"What is the number in the ones place in 845?"

Ending Sounds

Ending a lesson to assess understanding:
A recent kindergarten lesson on **ending sounds** used the following transition to dismiss the students.

"Name the ending sound that you hear.... bat, great, foot"
The teacher points to two students to answer and then they leave the group for the next activity.
"Name the ending sound that you hear.... hop, shape, trip"
The teacher again points to two students to answer and be dismissed. The transition continues until all have been dismissed.

Character Analysis

After a second grade **character analysis** lesson in which students created a mind map for the book *Ira Sleeps Over*, the students were asked:

"Please name one emotion or feeling that the main character had during the story." The teacher quickly moves in and out of the students gently touching each for a response. If no response comes, she simply

©KGF

says, "Think a minute and I will be right back." The teacher continues on and comes back to the child who is now ready with a repeat of an answer he heard or has come up with a new answer. If adept students are repeating others, the teacher may say, "Try to come up with one that hasn't been said and I will be right back to you."

Blast Off

The children count down actual seconds until everyone should be on the rug.
15, 14, 13, 12, ... Blast off!

Name It

"Name a continent." (country, state, capital)
"Name something found under the ground."
"Name something found in a grocery store."
"Name something you would wear in hot weather."
"Name a state of matter and point to a friend to name an example."
"Name something found in the freezer."
"Name a vegetable."
"Name a favorite author."
"Recommend a favorite book."

You get the idea!

Above/Below the Ground
Does it grow above or below ground?

(above)		(below)	
orange	broccoli	turnip	radish
tomato	lettuce	beet	garlic
pear	peach	carrot	peanut
cucumber	date	potato	onion
cauliflower	apple	parsnip	horseradish

What is It?

Use the students' names on cards. When you hold their name up (or spell the name) that student may go into the next activity as directed.

Variations: use shapes, numbers, letters, sounds, sight words, spelling words, presidents, capitals, science vocabulary, etc.

©Karen's Kids

Teacher Talk

I like to use popsicle question sticks. When a stick is pulled out of the can or cup, the students can be asked individually to answer or they can huddle in a group to come up the answer. When working in groups to answer, it is important to remember to keep a short waiting time or quick dismissal transition.

Becky Griffith – 2nd grade
SFASU 1984 and 1986

Popsicle Questions

Labels may be typed or printed and stuck on large colored popsicle sticks. These sticks may be placed in a container and kept close to the teacher's chair on the rug where the students gather for group times.

Ideas for sticks: months, days, states, words that need capitals, Continents, synonyms, antonyms, verbs, nouns, adjectives, money pieces and values, odd numbers, even numbers, + 2, - 2, +10, - 10, telephone numbers, zip codes, street address, book characters.

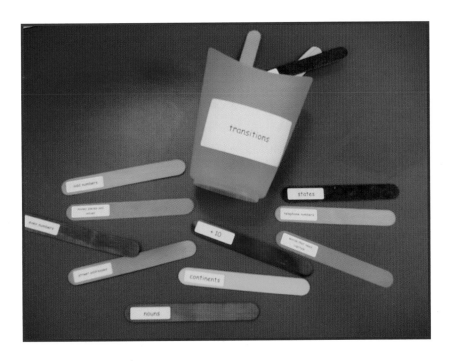

Roll Call Thinking
Waiting/Dismissal Transitions

Have the children answer the question to call roll or use as a transition instead of saying, "here or present".

...your last name
...your favorite smell
...something red
...something hard
...name of a President
...an animal that lives in the ocean
...something made of wood
...something oval shaped
...number greater than _____
...something that attracts to a magnet
...a three syllable word
...a word that rhymes with _____
...something that is green and long
...something that is soft, red, and big

You will find the children will help you think
of things at "thinking" time.

Teacher Talk

I love using the 'tune of' songs to give children information, get them to follow directions, or increase their vocabularies. Spelling words in a song or chant is a wonderful way to give directions while also providing an acceptable way for children to be verbal. Transitions should always teach or reinforce concepts.

Carolyn Davis – SFASU
SFASU 1977 and 1982

Spelling Transition Examples

Identify one word or phrase that is vital to the concept being constructed. Use that word or phrase throughout a lesson to gain or recapture attention. The number of letters in the word or words in the phrase dictates the tune.

Three letter words or three word phrases:
Row, Row, Row Your Boat or Three Blind Mice

Four letter words or phrases: Are You Sleeping

Five letter words or phrases: Bingo

Six letter words or phrases: Twinkle Twinkle Little Star

Concept: Solar System
Word: 'sun'
Tune: Three Blind Mice
S-U-N, S-U-N,
That spells sun,
That spells sun.
The sun is a star and is medium in size,
S-U-N, S-U-N (repeat getting softer each time until everyone is quiet)

Continued…

Concept: Plants
Word: leaf
Tune: Are You Sleeping
L-E-A-F, L-E-A-F, That spells leaf, That spells leaf. Leaves are parts of plants, They collect sunlight each day, Leaves are important, Leaves are important.

Concept: spelling sight words
Word: because

Tune: Twinkle, Twinkle Little Star
B-e-c-a-u-s-e, that's the way we spell because.
B-e-c-a-u-s-e, B-e-c-a-u-se, B-e-c-a-u-s-e, That's
the way we spell because.

Music and melodies have a way with sticking in our memories. What better way to help students retrieve facts and information?

Days of the Week
(Sung to the tune of the Adam's Family)

Days of the week. (snap, snap)
Days of the week. (snap, snap)
Days of the week, days of the week
Days of the week. (snap, snap)

There's Sunday and there's Monday
There's Tuesday and there's Wednesday
There's Thursday and there's Friday
And then there's Saturday.

Teaching

The Continent Song
(To the tune of *He's got the Whole World in His Hands*)

We've got the whole globe in our hands,
We've got the whole globe in our hands,
We've got the whole globe in our hands,
We've got the whole globe in our hands.

We've got North and South America in our hands,
We've got Europe, Asia, and Africa in our hands,
We've got Australia and Antarctica in our hands,
We've go the whole globe in our hands.

Number Rhyme
Taken from Jack Hartmann CD

Round and round and round we go when we get home we have a **zero**.

Start at the top and down we run that's the way we make a **one**.

Around and back on the railroad track! Two, two, **two**!

Around a tree, around a tree, that's the way we make **three**.

Down and over and down some more, that's the way we make a **four**.

Down and around with a flag on high, that's the way we make a **five**.

Around to a loop number **six** rolls a hoop.

Across the sky and down from heaven, that's the way we make a **seven**.

Make a S and do not wait when we get home we have **eight**.

Make a loop and then a line that the way we make a **nine**.

Now we have our number rhyme!

Things You Can Change or Cannot Change

Thinking and Reasoning—making quick decisions

1.	the clothes you wear	can change
2.	the color of your eyes	cannot change
3.	the weather	cannot change
4.	how neat your room is	can change
5.	the day of the week	cannot change
6.	the people you play with	can change
7.	the plants in a garden	can change
8.	having to go to school	cannot change
9.	the correct spelling of a word	cannot change
10.	the food you eat	cannot change
11.	how much something costs at the store	cannot change
12.	the number of hours in a day	cannot change
13.	your handwriting	can change
14.	the books you read	can change
15.	the sound made by thunder	cannot change
16.	what time the sun rises	cannot change
17.	how well you listen	can change
18.	how old you are	cannot change
19.	how strong you are	can change
20.	when summer will start	cannot change
21.	how much you weigh	can change
22.	when the tide comes in or goes out	cannot change
23.	how fast your bicycle goes	can change
24.	the amount of sleep you get	can change
25.	the rotation of the earth	cannot change

Instead of using a transition jingle, begin a circle game that children will WANT to join quickly. It can be understood that the new activity will begin when the song ends. Note: A 5 or 10 minute warning must have been given before the song begins.

Carolyn Abel
Elementary Education Department

Maximize Learning – Review Transitions

Select review songs to help cement learning. Example: Begin playing the **CIRCLE** song (Hap Palmer / #1). As children begin to notice the music, they clean up and come to the circle. When they arrive, the teacher hands them one of **TEN** color cards and they sit in the circle. When the song calls their **COLOR**, they follow the directions (stand up, sit down). The song continues, reviewing **COLORS.**

The "One Shape, Three shapes" song is another. This time, the teacher hands each child a **FELT SHAPE** and sets up a **FELT BOARD** at the front of the circle. They listen for the song to call their shape. The "Marching Around the Alphabet" song (#5) works well, also, but you would need to create an ABC circle for children to stand on as they parade around in a circle while singing this song. The "Number March" (#4) would also work nicely but the teacher would need to gently tap the correct number of students (later a child does the tapping) when the song requests two students, three, etc. Others include "The Circle" (Palmer) and "Numbers Rumba" (Raffi). Listen to them here (or google): **http://www.amazon.com/gp/recsradio/radio/ B00004TVSM/ref=pd_krex_listen_dp_img?ie=UTF8&refTagSuffix=dp_img**

OLDER CHILDREN: Use Chapin's song, "Great Big Words" (#20) only this time, students select from a group of multisyllabic **VOCABULARY WORDS** being studied that week. During the instrumental, children place their **WORD** into the correct **SENTENCE** that uses it "in context." An alternate format— match words with definitions. "Picnic of the World" (#24) teaches countries, but you would need to create a **HUGE WORLD MAP** for placing selected "countries." **http://www.amazon.com/gp/product/B000QJNR5K/ref=dm_ sp_adp**

Rhyme Away Stories

Draw a picture with coordinating colors and picture on a dry erase board. As you or the students read...leave out the _____ rhyming word you want them to say. Erase those items as you say the rhyme. You can also draw the picture as you go instead of erasing it. Make up your own!

If you can clap real loud, erase a <u>cloud</u>.

If you can see a shoe, erase the color <u>blue</u>.

If you can rub your head, erase the color <u>red</u>.

Stand up and touch your back, now erase the color <u>black</u>.

You look like a really nice fellow. Now erase the color <u>yellow</u>.

Make the funniest face ever seen...now erase the color <u>green</u>.

My cousin's name is Urcle, he likes the color <u>purple</u>.

With a loud clap, loud clap, loud...erase the very last <u>cloud</u>.

Rhyme Away Story by:
Cay McAninch 2002

The possibilities for content-teaching related transitions are endless and are NOT limited. Use your imagination and experiences to help assess, review, and teach while using those short times in the day to move into another activity or area.

The 50 States That Rhyme Song
(To the tune of *Turkey in the Straw*)

Alabama, and Alaska, Arizona, Arkansas
California, Colorado, Co-nnecticut and more
Delaware, Florida, Georgia, Hawaii, Idaho
Illinois, Indi-a-na, I-o-wa

Kansas, and Kentucky, Louisiana, Maine
Maryland, Massachusetts and good old Michigan
Minnesota, Mississippi, Missouri, and Montana
Nebraska's 27, number 28's Nevada

Next, New Hampshire, and New Jersey, and way down, New Mexico
There's New York, North Carolina, North Dakota, Ohio
Oklahoma, Oregon, Pennsylvania, now let's see
Rhode Island, South Carolina, South Dakota, Tennessee

Texas and there's Utah, Vermont, I'm almost through
Virginia and there's Washington, and West Virginia, too
Could Wisconsin be the last state or is it just 49?
No, Wyoming is the last state in The 50 States That Rhyme!

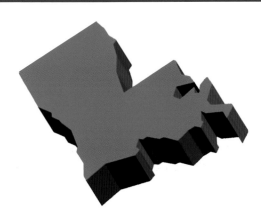

Phonemic Awareness

© Karen G Frandsen 2001

Phonemic awareness transitions can be used as needed for waiting, dismissal, or small group activities, and may be adjusted for the appropriate age group.

BLENDING PHONEMES

"B----A----T"

Call three or four children to the front of the rug to form a football huddle. The teacher says, "/b/—/a/—/t/." The children say, "BAT!" and are dismissed from the rug.

©KGF

If You Think You Know This Word
(To the tune of If *You're Happy and You Know It*)

If you think you know this word, raise your hand.
If you think you know this word, raise your hand.
If you think you know this word, if you think you know this word,
If you think you know this word, raise your hand.

The teacher says, "/ch/—/ee/—/se/," calls on a child, and the child says, "CHEESE!" The child is dismissed to the next activity.

Variations:
Choose other actions children can do to indicate they know the word: marshmallow clap or close their eyes.

Dry-Erase Boards with Counters

Each child has a dry-erase board and counters. The teacher writes a sentence and the class stomps the number of words (or claps syllables) in the sentence. Children are asked to visually represent the number of words in the sentence by placing the appropriate number of counters on the dry-erase board.

Spring   is   almost   here.

Pocket Chart Stomp!

Write a sentence on a sentence strip: _____ likes to eat pizza. Xavier is called to the group rug and asked to insert the name card of a friend into the blank. The class reads the sentence while stomping the number of words in the sentence.

	Tameka	likes	to	eat	pizza.
stomp	X	X	X	X	X

Xavier is dismissed to learning centers and Tameka comes to the front of the room and chooses a friend's name to be placed in the sentence. Continue this activity until all friends are dismissed.

After children are comfortable stomping words, make the lesson more challenging by having them clap syllables.

	Ta	me	ka	likes	to	eat	piz	za.
clap	X	X	X	X	X	X	X	X

©KGF

LETTER SOUNDS

B—A—Bay

B—A—bay,
B—E—bee,
B—I—bikki—bye,
B—O—Bow,
Bikki—bye—bow—B—U—boo
Bikki—bye—bow—boo!

Substitute consonants.
(from the Three Stooges)

I Like to Eat

I like to eat! I like to eat! I like to eat, eat, apples and bananas.
I like to eat! I like to eat! I like to eat, eat, apples and bananas.

Substitute vowels **A E I O U**

A Aey lake tay ate! Aye lake tay ate! Aye lake tay ate, ate, apeles and bay-nay-nays.
Aey lake tay ate! Aye lake tay ate! Aye lake tay ate, ate, apeles and baynaynays.

O Oh loke toe oat! Oh loke toe oat. Oh loke toe oat, oat opples and bow-no-nos
Oh loke toe oat! Oh loke toe oat. Oh loke to oat, oat opeles and bow-no-nos.

Continue with all vowels.
A E I O U

Have you Ever Seen a Dog on a Log?
(To the tune of If You're Happy and You Know It)

Have you ever seen a dog on a log?
Have you ever seen a dog on a log?
No, I've never, never, never...
No, I've never, never, never...
No, I've never seen a dog on a log.

Substitute other rhyming words for the underlined words.

Corner Grocery Store

There were plums, plums, sucking on their thumbs,
At the store, at the store.
There were plums, plums, sucking on their thumbs,
At the corner grocery store.

There was corn, corn, blowing on the horn.
At the store, at the store.
There was corn, corn, blowing on the horn.
At the corner grocery store.

Substitute other foods and phrases that rhyme.

SEGMENTING by PHONEMES

Beginning Sounds

Choose a picture with a single object on it. There should be one card for each beginning sound of the children's names in the classroom. Hold up a picture card of one object and sing (to the tune of Skip to My Lou),

Whose name starts like this…?
Whose name starts like this…?
Whose name starts like this…picture that I'm holding?

Children are dismissed when a picture that begins with the letter that starts their name is shown.

(Make sure your pictures match the beginning sounds of a child's name. For Charity, you might choose a picture of a cherry—ch.
For Thad, you might choose a picture of a thimble.

Old McDonald

(Remember - Be careful when saying consonant sounds NOT to add a vowel at the end. DO NOT say "buh, buh, buh" for "b-b-b." Let the consonant sound roll off your lips and cut it short.)

What's the sound that starts these words: 'dog,' 'did,' and 'dad'?
What's the sound that starts these words: 'dog,' 'did,' and 'dad'?
With a 'd-d' here, and a 'd-d';
Here a 'd-d,' there a 'd-d,' everywhere a 'd-d,' 'd-d'
What's the sound that starts these words: 'dog,' 'did,' and 'dad'?

Children say, "D!"

Willoughby, Wallaby, Woo

Willoughby, Wallaby, Woo,
An elephant sat on you!
Willoughby, Wallaby, Wee,
An elephant sat on me.

Each child's name is written on a sentence strip and cut to length of the name. Write beginning capital consonant letters to be used in the song on sentence strips. Cut to length. Insert the child's name in a pocket chart. Right before you sing the verse, insert the beginning consonant card over the first letter of the child's name. If the child's name begins with a vowel, insert the beginning letter immediately to the left of the first letter in the name.

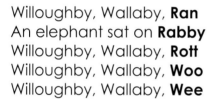

Willoughby, Wallaby, **Ran**	An elephant sat on **Jan**!
An elephant sat on **Rabby**	An elephant sat on **Abby**!
Willoughby, Wallaby, **Rott**	An elephant sat on **Scott**!
Willoughby, Wallaby, **Woo**	An elephant sat on **YOU**!
Willoughby, Wallaby, **Wee**	An elephant sat on **ME**!

A-B-C Names

This activity is challenging!! Be careful when saying consonant sounds NOT to add a vowel at the end. DO NOT say "buh, buh, buh" for "b-b-b." Let the consonant sound roll off your lips and cut it short.

Clap 1-2-3 while saying, "B-B-Bob."

Clap 1-2-3-4 while saying "D-D-Dus-tin."

As children's names are clapped, they are dismissed to the next activity.

WORD and SYLLABLES

Stomping Words and Clapping Syllables

Call a small group of children to the front of the group time rug. Ask them to get into a football huddle and listen to the sentence: "Tomorrow is our field trip."

Children are to huddle together, repeat the sentence, and <u>stomp</u> the number of words in the sentence.

	Tomorrow	is	our	field	trip.
stomp	X	X	X	X	X

Call one child to the front of the group and say, "Choose your center Brandon." Brandon stomps each word as he replies, "I choose the library center." Brandon is dismissed to the library center.

After children are comfortable stomping words, make the lesson more challenging by having them clap syllables. (It is important to note that children should use one action for WORDS and another for syllables, so as not to confuse them.)

	To	mor	row	is	our	field	trip.
clap	X	X	X	X	X	X	X

Clapping Syllables

Children need to hear the number of claps in many words. The easiest word for them to hear the syllables is in their name and the names of friends and family. After practicing as a group, a simple dismissal can be executed.

"If your name is a one clap name, you may …"
"If your name is a two clap name, you may …"

This activity may be varied by saying, "I am going to clap your name. When you hear your name clapped, you may…"

Who Has It?
(To the tune of *Jimmy Crack Corn*)

(This activity is challenging!! Be careful when saying consonant sounds NOT to add a vowel at the end. DO NOT say "buh, buh, buh" for "b-b-b." Let the consonant sound roll off your lips and cut it short.)

Children sit in a circle. The teacher places a very small object in one child's hand, making sure no one else sees the object.
Sing,

"Who has a 'b' (sing sound) think to share?
"Who has a 'b' thing to share?
"Who has a 'b' thing to share?
"It must begin with 'b'!"

Row, Row, Row, Your Boat

Row, row, row your boat,
Gently down the stream.
Merrily, merrily, merrily, merrily,
Life is but a dream.
Change merrily to
berrily
derrily
ferrily
smerrily
therrily

You may want to use a pocket chart for this activity and place the different beginning consonants/blends/digraphs over the 'm' in merrily.

I CAN'T SPELL HIPPOPOTAMUS

I can spell CAT   C-A-T.
I can spell RAT   R-A-T.
I can spell MAT   M-A-T.
But I can't spell hippopotamus!

Chorus: H-I-P-P-O-I know, and then comes P-O-T
    But that's as far as I can go, and that's what bothers me-GEE
    "Hey" I can spell hippopotamus!

I can spell DOG   D-O-G.
I can spell HOG   H-O-G.
I can spell LOG   L-O-G.
But I can't spell hippopotamus!

Chorus: H-I-P-P-O-I know, and then comes P-O-T
    But that's as far as I can go, and that's what bothers me-GEE
    "Hey" I can spell hippopotamus!

I can spell RED   R-E-D.
I can spell BED   B-E-D.
I can spell TED   T-E-D.
But I can't spell hippopotamus!

Chorus: H-I-P-P-O-I know, and then comes P-O-T
    But that's as far as I can go, and that's what bothers me-GEE
    "Hey" I can spell hippopotamus!

Make cards to hold up with word written on them. Make up more verses with other chunks on them to help see and hear the rhymes.

Phonemic Awareness

What's Missing?

Write a sentence on the sentence strip. Ask the children how many words are in the sentence. Cut the words apart as the class counts them (i.e. "Humpty Dumpty sat on a wall. This sentence has six words."). Six children are selected as helpers. Each child holds a word from the cut sentence strip and stands in correct order to reconstruct the sentence so children can read it. The remaining children close their eyes. The teacher chooses one child by tapping him/her on the shoulder. This is a signal for this child to turn around backwards so her word can no longer be read. Children are instructed to open their eyes and are asked to guess the missing word. (This is an excellent transitions for a long waiting time or a rainy day.)

Humpty		sat	on	the	wall

Rhyme Time

Children are to listen for the word that does not belong. The teacher calls on a child and says four words: three words rhyme and one does not. Be careful to not always say the "odd" word at the beginning or at the end. Children will listen to the pattern if the odd word is always at the end rather than the rhyming words.

1. fat, rat, crack, bat   (crack)
2. stop, top, hop, tap   (tap)

_____ and _____ are rhyming words, rhyming words
_____ and _____ are rhyming words, they sound a lot a like.

Dismissal

Dismissal transitions are used to shift and move any age child, in an orderly fashion, to the next location or activity of your choice. Children may be dismissed individually or several at a time, depending on the teacher's needs.

Bee, Bee, Bumblebee

Bee, Bee, Bumblebee.
Stung a man upon his knee.
Stung a pig upon his snout.
One, two three, let's go out.

(Tap one child on the head as you say, "One, two, three."
These three children are dismissed to centers, snack, the
bathroom, or outside.)

Consonant Sounds

Pass out cards with pictures on them. Make sure the pictures are not
representative of blends or digraphs (cherry, truck, shoe, plate, etc.).

If you have a picture that begins with 'B,' you may...

...walk to the door.
...choose your center.
...go eat lunch.

(It is understood that the child will bring his/her picture to the teacher before
leaving the rug.)

Is it Real?

Pass out cards with pictures of real objects and make-believe objects.
Label two boxes and place them on the rug next to the teacher. Call
children one at a time and have the place their picture in the appropriate
box.

Variation:
Sort a variety of pictures:
       fiction and non-fiction
       eat and don't eat
       poison and not poison

Teacher Talk

"It is important to support positive peer relations with upper elementary school students. This is the time when cliques and bullying can immerge if quality peer interactions are not supported and facilitated. The following transition offers an opportunity to dismiss students in pair, while fostering appreciation for quality character traits of peers."

**Erica S. Dillard,
Instructor-Elementary Ed
SFASU 1996 & 2001**

The Name/Character Trait Dismissal

At the beginning of the school year, each student creates a name card. The teacher selects half of the cards and places them in the pocket chart. He/She then uses the remaining cards to call on students. The student called by the teacher selects a peer's name card from the pocket chart. The student offers an affirmation of a positive character trait for the peer selected. Both students then dismiss together. (If time allows both students my offer affirmations for each other.) This is continued until all students are dismissed. When there is an odd number of students in the classroom, the teacher offers the affirmation. By randomly drawing the cards each time, students will be placed in a situation to offer an affirmation for a new peer during each experience in which this dismissal is utilized by the classroom teacher.

Bye-Bye
(To the tune of *Let's Go Riding in a Car, Car*)

Jeff and Andrew, please stand up.
Brady and Brandon, please stand up.
Holly and Becky, please stand up.
It's time to _____ now.

(Fill in the blank with where you want the children to go. You may choose to only dismiss two children at a time, in which case you would repeat their names rather than adding new names.)

Teacher Talk

*It is important to support positive peer relations with upper elementary school students. This is the time when cliques and bullying can immerge if quality peer interactions are not supported and facilitated. **Zap Tapper** offers an opportunity to dismiss students in pair, while fostering appreciation for quality character traits of peers.*

Erica S. Dillard
SFASU 1996 & 2001

Zap Tapper

The teacher makes a "zap tapper" from a variety of objects:

dust mop with jiggly eyes, felt nose and mouth, and a ribbon for hair-shaped fly swatter with jiggly eyes, felt nose, mouth

The teacher creates a rhyme to go with the zap tapper. One child is the "zapper" and as the class chants the rhyme, the zapper "zaps" children on the head. As a child is zapped, he or she leaves the rug.

Come Follow

Come follow, follow, follow,
Come follow, follow, me.
Come follow, follow, follow,
Come follow, follow, me.

Take one step. (Children take one step)
Take baby steps. (Children take baby steps.)

Come follow, follow, follow
Come follow, follow, me.

Recognizing....

...printed names

...shapes

...colors

...parents' names

...last name

...birthday

Sleeping

Sprinkle the students with imaginary sleeping dust.
They all pretend to fall asleep and you sing

"Wake up sleepy Lauren.
Wake up sleepy Ethan.
Wake up sleepy Kole and walk to the line."

***Variation:* Sing – The Lazy Mary Song**
(substitute the children's names)

Lazy <u>Mary</u> will you get up?
Will you get up?
Will you get up?
Lazy <u>Mary</u> will you get up?
Will you get up?
Will you get up and line up at the door...go to _____ ?

©KGF

Get on Board

I've got a friend that you all know and _____ is his/her name.
I've got a friend that you all know and _____ is his/her name.
Get on board, little _____, get on board, little _____,
Get on board, little _____.
It's time for library _____. (to go outside) (to go to lunch).

Cracker and Crumbs

Cracker and crumbs
Cracker and crumbs
These are my fingers and
These are my thumbs.

Stones and books
Stones and books
Come a little closer and
Take a look.

Eyes

When my eyes meet your eyes, you may …

…go to the door.
…get your lunch.
…wash your hands.

Skip to My Lou
(To the tune of Skip to my Lou)

Skip, skip, skip to the door.
Skip, skip, skip to the door.
Skip, skip, skip to the door.
It's time to go outside.

Variation:
Change to word "skip" to other action words:
jump, hop, slither, bounce, slide, skate, etc.

If Your Name Begins with the Letter I Sing

If your name begins with the letter I sing, stand up! Stand up! '**B**.'
If your name begins with the letter '**B**', you may.....

    ...go outside.
    ...walk to the bathroom.
    ...jump to your center.

Variation:

The teacher holds up a capital letter and says, "If your name begins with this letter, you may..."

Snail, Snail

Snail, snail, come out and get fed
First your feelers, then your head.
Then your momma and your papa
We'll feed you fried mutton.
(repeat as often as necessary)

Children hold hands and move in a circle, forming a spiral. They turn and come out of the spiral into a circle again, then move to the door.

If You're Happy and You Know It
(To the tune of If You're Happy and You Know It)

If you're happy and you know it, stand right up.
If you're happy and you know it, stand right up.
If you're happy and you know it, then your face will surely show it,
If you're happy and you know it, walk outside.

If you're ready to each lunch, stand right up.
If you're ready to each lunch, stand right up.
If you're ready to each lunch, and you really want to munch,
If you're ready to each lunch, walk to the door.

Teacher Talk

This transition, **A Tisket, a Tasket**, is so short and simple and helps the children learn to recognize their names, as well as their friends' names. This is a great quick literacy activity to use with young children.

Brenda Bowline – Pre-K II
SFASU, 2007

A Tisket, a Tasket

Teacher says: "A tisket, a tasket,
Whose names are in my basket?"

Have all of the children's name tags in a basket. Hold up one, two, or three name tags at a time as you sing the song. When the children recognize their names, they will come up and get their name tags and go to learning centers.

Variations: Start with the children's first names on their name tags at the beginning of the year. After Christmas, put only their last names on the name tags. It is amazing how quickly they will recognize not only their last names, but their friend's last names, too!

Nah, Nah

Nah, nah…nah, nah, nah, nah…
Hey, Hey, **stand up**.
Nah, nah…nah, nah, nah, nah…
Hey, Hey, **get in line**.

Variation: Substitute any word needed to give instructions on where and how to go there.

My toddlers love getting their turn to catch and roll the ball back. I use this transition after group time to dismiss them outside.

Louann Williams - Toddler I
SFASU, 1979

I Roll the Ball

"I roll the ball across the floor
Until it lands at _____ door."
child's name

Roll the ball to the child. When the ball reaches the child, he rolls the ball back to the teacher and is dismissed. Repeat until all children are dismissed.

Variations: *Older children can roll the ball to each other to free your time to manage the children lining up or going to another location.*

• use a car or a truck to roll
• emphasize the color of the object that is being rolled

If you...

"If you can hear my words, _____." Use any command: stand up, walk to the door, turn and face your neighbor.

Huddle Up

Teacher calls several children to come to the front. She asks a question, and the children huddle up to talk about the answer. Once the answer is given, children are dismissed to the next activity.

Teacher Talk

My toddlers love getting their turn to catch and roll the ball back. I use this transition after group time to dismiss them outside.

Louann Williams - Toddler I
SFASU, 1979

Jack-in-the-Box

Children crouch on the rug. When their name is called, they jump up and repeat:

Teacher:	**Jack -in-the-box,** **Oh, so still.** **Won't you come out?**
Child:	**Yes! I will!!**

Substitute each child's name for Jack. As a name is called, he/she jumps up and says, "Yes I will," and goes to the desired location.

Variation:

When you need to dismiss several at a time say:

Jack in the box – Sally in the box, Justin in the box oh so still.
Won't you all come out?
They all jump up and say, "We will!"

Attributes

Using students' clothes, hair, eyes, etc., find several students who have like attributes. Ask them to make a group in the middle of the rug. Students must then look closely and see what that group has in common. The more attributes you use at a time...the harder it becomes. EXAMPLE: 3 children who have red hair, shirts with letters on them, and all 3 have on sandals. This can be used for waiting or dismissal.

Mystery Child

The teacher describes the physical characteristics of the "mystery" child, including the child's clothing. Children guess who the mystery child is. The mystery child describes a classmate. After the class guesses the second mystery child, the child who did the describing leaves the rug.

Oh, Do You Know What Time it Is?
(To the tune of Muffin Man)

Oh, do you know what time it is?
What time it is? What time it is?
Oh, do you know what time it is?
It's time to go ...

...to the library.
...outside.
...for a walk.

Lazy Mary Will You Get Up?

Lazy Mary will you get up? Will you get up? Will you get up?
Lazy Mary will you get up? And _____

...choose your center.
...hop to the door.
...tiptoe outside.

Substitute children's names until all children are dismissed.

Teacher Talk

This transition works well with any age children. Choose your focus for the transition to help reinforce or assess students in particular areas.

Crystal Williams
SFASU

Flash Light Stars

Turn out the lights. When the flashlight focuses on the child he will tell you a letter in his name and then he may line up, sit at the table, etc.

Variation: *Let them find a shape in the room, a letter, numbers, etc. Let if fit whatever concept you are working on.*

Older students: When the flashlight shines on you, tell me the capital of _____.

Mate Match

Materials needed are:
- construction paper squares
- tongue depressor lollipops with upper case letters on one set
- and lower case letters on the other

Children find their "mate." The pairs are dismissed.

Variation:
number of dots to the numeral
shapes
color

Where is Andrew?
(To the tune of *Where is Thumbkin?*)

Teacher:	Where is Andrew? Where is Andrew?
Andrew:	Here I am. Here I am.
Teacher:	How are you today, sir?
Andrew:	Very well, I thank you.
Teacher:	Hop to the door. Hop to the door.

The teacher chooses a different way for each child to move to the door, choose centers, etc.

Who Do You See?
(To the tune of *Brown Bear, Brown Bear*)

Teacher:	Amber, Amber, who do you see?
Amber:	I see Clint looking at me.
Class Sings:	Clint, Clint, who do you see?
Clint:	I see Carrie looking at me.

Continue singing until all children are dismissed.

©Karen's Kids

Teacher Talk

*I used **Now It's Time** with my Kindergarten students the very first day of school. It is a transition that is easy to remember and easy to modify. I use this transition for lunch time, going to the restroom, water breaks, cleaning up after centers, etc. As this transition became familiar to students, they soon began to help transition each other.*

Larry Cupit -Kindergarten
SFASU 2003 and 2005

Now It's Time
(To the tune of Mary had a Little Lamb)

Now it's time to go outside, go outside, go outside,
Now it's time to go outside, Steven and Helen may go.

Substitute names until all children are dismissed.

Rhyme Time

Children are to listen for the word that does not belong. The teacher calls on a child and says four words: three words rhyme and one does not. Be careful to not always say the "odd" word at the beginning or at the end. Children will listen to the pattern (the word is always at the end) rather than the words.

1.   fat, rat, crack, bat (crack)
2.   stop, top, hop, tap (tap)

_____ and _____ are rhyming words, rhyming words
_____ and _____ are rhyming words, they sound a lot alike.